Fun
BIBLE
SUDOKU

2

Fun
BIBLE
SUDOKU

2

BARBOUR
PUBLISHING

ISBN 978-1-59789-861-4

Published by Barbour Publishing, Inc., P.O. Box 719, Uhrichsville, Ohio 44683, www.barbourbooks.com

Our mission is to publish and distribute inspirational products offering exceptional value and biblical encouragement to the masses.

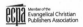

Member of the
Evangelical Christian
Publishers Association

Printed in the United States of America.

WELCOME TO THE WORLD OF **BIBLE SUDOKU**!

Millions worldwide have discovered the joy of sudoku—the puzzle that tests your skills of logic. The rapid growth in sudoku's popularity has rightly been called a phenomenon.

But what in the world is "Bible sudoku"? We're glad you asked!

Fun Bible Sudoku 2 combines the enjoyment of solving a sudoku puzzle with the challenge of Bible trivia. First, you put your Bible knowledge to the test, solving scripture-based clues to determine either the numerical or letter-based "givens" for each puzzle. Then you prove your logic abilities by completing the sudoku grid.

Here's how it works exactly:

Number-based puzzles

1. Each puzzle begins with a blank 9 x 9 grid. A coordinate system—with the letters A through I across the top and the numbers 1 through 9 down the left side—will help you place the "givens," or starter numbers, generated by the Bible trivia questions.
2. For each puzzle, trivia questions will be answered by the numbers 1 through 9. The coordinates with each question (for example, *A1, C9, H3*) indicate where you should insert that particular answer into the sudoku grid. If you don't know the answer and want to find out from the Bible, references are provided. Or if you're really eager to get started, the answers are shown, upside down, underneath the puzzle grid.
3. Once you've inserted the givens into the grid, you can solve the sudoku puzzle. The goal of sudoku is to place the numbers 1 through 9 in each row, each column, and each of nine 3 x 3 minigrids (the shaded areas) within the larger puzzle. Numbers can never be duplicated in a row, column, or 3 x 3 grid—so use your skills of deduction to determine what numbers can or can't go into a particular box.

Letter-based puzzles

1. Each 9 x 9 grid includes "givens," as with traditional sudoku puzzles. But in this case, the givens are letters. The nine letters in each row, column, and 3 x 3 minigrid will spell out a biblical word or phrase. Each word or phrase is taken directly from the King James Version of the Bible, unless a "/" is seen, in which case a modern equivalent is used in the puzzle. For example, "to keep/_____ the way" indicates that the KJV term "keep" will be replaced by another word; the context of the puzzle should help you determine the correct usage.
2. Each puzzle has a hint with a reference beneath it.
3. Letter-based puzzles are solved in the same manner as the number-based sudoku. Instead of using nine different numbers, you will use nine different letters. When solving, make sure that no letter repeats within any row, within any column, or within any of the nine 3 x 3 minigrids.

Special thanks to our puzzle designer, Sara Stoker.
We hope you enjoy *Fun Bible Sudoku 2*!

	A	B	C	D	E	F	G	H	I
1	R	D	D	S	e	F	I	o	O
2	I	O	F	d	r	h	s	E	l
3	H	e	S	O	i	L	R	d	F
4	F	D	E	i	O	r	L	S	h
5	L	R	O	t	H	S	E	I	D
6	S	H	i	e	L	d	f	o	r
7	O	S	R	H	f	E	D	l	I
8	D	F	H	I	S	i	O	R	e
9	E	i	L	R	d	O	H	F	S

Hint: Row 6

But thou, O Lord, art a ꟷshield for ꟷ me. (Psalm 3:3)

PUZZLE 2
Easy

For A3, E4, G5
For many deceivers are entered into the world, who confess not that Jesus Christ is come in the flesh. This is a deceiver and an antichrist. (2 John 1:_)

For A7, B2, D9, E6, F1, H5
Set your affection on things above, not on things on the earth. (Colossians 3:_)

For B1, E5, G6
And the second angel sounded, and as it were a great mountain burning with fire was cast into the sea: and the third part of the sea became blood. (Revelation 8:_)

For B4, C8, D1, F5, I3
Yet for love's sake I rather beseech thee, being such an one as Paul the aged, and now also a prisoner of Jesus Christ. (Philemon _)

For B5, D7, E2, H9
But now hath he obtained a more excellent ministry, by how much also he is the mediator of a better covenant, which was established upon better promises. (Hebrews 8:_)

For B8, C2, D3, H1
Christ is become of no effect unto you, whosoever of you are justified by the law; ye are fallen from grace. (Galatians 5:_)

For B9, C6, D5, E8, F3, H2, I7
Then Jerubbaal, who is Gideon, and all the people that were with him, rose up early, and pitched beside the well of Harod. (Judges 7:_)

For C5, F7, G2, H8
And the second angel poured out his vial upon the sea; and it became as the blood of a dead man: and every living soul died in the sea. (Revelation 16:_)

For F9, G8, H4
Having a form of godliness, but denying the power thereof: from such turn away. (2 Timothy 3:_)

	A	B	C	D	E	F	G	H	I
1	7	2	8	9	6	7	1	3	5
2		2							
3	7								
4		9			1				
5					8		7	2	
6					2		8		
7	2								
8			9						
9				2					

Fun BIBLE **SUDOKU 2**

PUZZLE 3
Easy

For A1, C7, D3, E8, F6, H2, I5
So king Solomon was king over all Israel. (1 Kings 4:1)

For A3, D2, G4, H8, I1
And when the queen of Sheba had seen all Solomon's wisdom, and the house that he had built. . . (1 Kings 10:2)

For A4, B1, D6, H5, I7
The Lord knoweth how to deliver the godly out of temptations, and to reserve the unjust unto the day of judgment to be punished. (2 Peter 2:1)

For A5, C3, D4, F9
Who then is Paul, and who is Apollos, but ministers by whom ye believed, even as the Lord gave to every man? (1 Corinthians 3:_)

For A7, C6, D8, E5, F2, H9
Even as the testimony of Christ was confirmed in you. . .
(1 Corinthians 1:_)

For A9, B5, D1, F8, G3, I6
But we were gentle among you, even as a nurse cherisheth her children. (1 Thessalonians 2:_)

For B2, F1, G7, I3
And having food and raiment let us be therewith content.
(1 Timothy 6:_)

For B8, C4, F7, G6, H1, I9
And be not conformed to this world: but be ye transformed by the renewing of your mind, that ye may prove what is that good, and acceptable, and perfect, will of God. (Romans 12:_)

For B9, E2, F4
And not only so, but we glory in tribulations also: knowing that tribulation worketh patience. (Romans 5:_)

	A	B	C	D	E	F	G	H	I
1	1	9		7		8		2	4
2		8		4	3	6		1	
3	4		5	1			7		8
4	9		2	5		3	4		
5	5	7			6			9	1
6			6			1	2		7
7	6		1	9		2	8		9
8		2		6	1	7		4	
9	7	3				5		6	2

Starter Numbers in Order:
1, 4, 9, 5, 6, 7, 8, 2, 3

For A1, C5, H3
For I am jealous over you with godly jealousy: for I have espoused you to one husband, that I may present you as a chaste virgin to Christ. (2 Corinthians 11:_)

For A3, B5, D8, E6
And they sing the song of Moses the servant of God, and the song of the Lamb, saying, Great and marvellous are thy works, Lord God Almighty. (Revelation 15:_)

For A6, F5, G2, H4, I7
Insomuch that we desired Titus, that as he had begun, so he would also finish in you the same grace also. (2 Corinthians 8:_)

For A7, C3, F2, G8, I5
And it came to pass, when they were gone over, that Elijah said unto Elisha, Ask what I shall do for thee, before I be taken away from thee. And Elisha said, I pray thee, let a double portion of thy spirit be upon me. (2 Kings 2:_)

For A9, F7, G1, H8
For God hath not given us the spirit of fear; but of power, and of love, and of a sound mind. (2 Timothy 1:_)

For B1, C6, D2, E4, F9, H5, I3
In the beginning God created the heaven and the earth. (Genesis 1:_)

For B4, C8, D9, G5, H7, I1
For it came to pass, when Solomon was old, that his wives turned away his heart after other gods: and his heart was not perfect with the LORD his God, as was the heart of David his father. (1 Kings 11:_)

For B7, D5, E1, H6, I9
Remember that Jesus Christ of the seed of David was raised from the dead according to my gospel. (2 Timothy 2:_)

For B8, C1, F3
For as the sufferings of Christ abound in us, so our consolation also aboundeth by Christ. (2 Corinthians 1:_)

	A	B	C	D	E	F	G	H	I
1									
2									
3									
4									
5									
6									
7									
8									
9									

Starter Numbers in Order:
2, 3, 6, 9, 7, 1, 4, 8, 5

PUZZLE 5
Easy

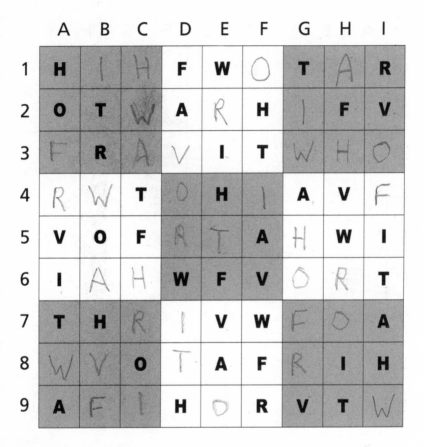

	A	B	C	D	E	F	G	H	I
1	H	I	H	F	W	O	T	A	R
2	O	T	W	A	R	H	I	F	V
3	F	R	A	V	I	T	W	H	O
4	R	W	T	O	H	I	A	V	F
5	V	O	F	R	T	A	H	W	I
6	I	A	H	W	F	V	O	R	T
7	T	H	R	I	V	W	F	O	A
8	W	V	O	T	A	F	R	I	H
9	A	F	I	H	O	R	V	T	W

Hint: Column D

And the boy Samuel continued to grow in stature and in _____
____ the LORD and with men. (1 Samuel 2:26 NIV)

	A	B	C	D	E	F	G	H	I
1	S	O	M	E	T	H	I	N	G
2	I	E	T	G	N	S	M	O	H
3	H	N	G	O	M	I	S	T	E
4	E	S	N	I	O	M	G	H	T
5	M	G	H	T	S	N	E	I	O
6	O	T	I	H	E	G	N	M	S
7	N	M	O	S	H	E	T	G	I
8	T	I	S	M	G	O	H	E	N
9	G	H	E	N	I	T	O	S	M

Hint: Row 1

Jesus replied, "They do not need to go away. You give them
_____ to eat." (Matthew 14:16 NIV)

PUZZLE 7
Easy

For A1, B7, D3, G2
And it shall be, that thou shalt drink of the brook; and I have commanded the ravens to feed thee there. (1 Kings 17:_)

For A3, C9, D5, F1, G4, H2, I7
And cast him into the bottomless pit, and shut him up, and set a seal upon him, that he should deceive the nations no more, till the thousand years should be fulfilled. (Revelation 20:_)

For A4, D8, F3, G6, I9
Then sang Deborah and Barak the son of Abinoam on that day, saying. . . (Judges 5:_)

For A5, B8, E7, F2, G1, H9, I6
Honour thy father and mother; which is the first commandment with promise. (Ephesians 6:_)

For A8, C1, D9
Circumcised the eighth day, of the stock of Israel, of the tribe of Benjamin, an Hebrew of the Hebrews; as touching the law, a Pharisee. . . (Philippians 3:_)

For B1, C8, E4, F7, G9, H3, I5
Now as Jannes and Jambres withstood Moses, so do these also resist the truth: men of corrupt minds, reprobate concerning the faith. (2 Timothy 3:_)

For C2, E6, H8
For in Jesus Christ neither circumcision availeth any thing, nor uncircumcision; but faith which worketh by love. (Galatians 5:_)

For C4, E3, G7, H5
I have fought a good fight, I have finished my course, I have kept the faith. (2 Timothy 4:_)

For C6, D7, F5, I2
If we confess our sins, he is faithful and just to forgive us our sins, and to cleanse us from all unrighteousness. (1 John 1:_)

	A	B	C	D	E	F	G	H	I
1									
2									
3									
4									
5									
6									
7									
8									
9									

Starter Numbers in Order:
4, 3, 1, 2, 5, 8, 6, 7, 9

PUZZLE 8
Easy

For A1, B6, C8
In this was manifested the love of God toward us, because that
God sent his only begotten Son into the world, that we might live
through him. (1 John 4:_)

For A3, C7, D4, F9, G6, I8
Henceforth there is laid up for me a crown of righteousness,
which the Lord, the righteous judge, shall give me at that day.
(2 Timothy 4:_)

For A6, C3, D2, G1, H8
And after Abimelech there arose to defend Israel Tola the son of
Puah. (Judges 10:_)

For A7, C1, D3, E6, F8
He that keepeth his mouth keepeth his life: but he that openeth
wide his lips shall have destruction. (Proverbs 13:_)

For A9, E8, F1, G3, H4, I7
So that ye were ensamples to all that believe in Macedonia and
Achaia. . . (1 Thessalonians 1:_)

For B9, C6, F7
And because ye are sons, God hath sent forth the Spirit of his Son
into your hearts, crying, Abba, Father. (Galatians 4:_)

For C2, D9, E5, I1
And it came to pass, afore Isaiah was gone out into the middle court,
that the word of the LORD came to him saying. . . (2 Kings 20:_)

For C4, E1, G9, H5, I2
Your riches are corrupted, and your garments are motheaten.
(James 5:_)

For F4, H7, I6
And the Lord direct your hearts into the love of God, and into the
patient waiting for Christ. (2 Thessalonians 3:_)

	A	B	C	D	E	F	G	H	I
1									
2									
3									
4									
5									
6									
7									
8									
9									

Starter Numbers in Order:
9, 8, 1, 3, 7, 6, 4, 2, 5

PUZZLE 9
Easy

For A1, E7, I4
Sound speech, that cannot be condemned; that he that is of the contrary part may be ashamed, having no evil thing to say of you. . . (Titus 2:_)

For A3, B4, H5
And the children of Israel again did evil in the sight of the LORD, when Ehud was dead. (Judges 4:_)

For A5, B1, C9, D6, F3, G4, I7
The eyes of the LORD are in every place, beholding the evil and the good. (Proverbs 15:_)

For A8, F1, I3
In all things shewing thyself a pattern of good works: in doctrine shewing uncorruptness, gravity, sincerity. . . (Titus 2:_)

For A9, B6, E5, F8
Being confident of this very thing, that he which hath begun a good work in you will perform it until the day of Jesus Christ. (Philippians 1:_)

For B5, C3, E2, F9, G8, H1, I6
As newborn babes, desire the sincere milk of the word, that ye may grow thereby. (1 Peter 2:_)

For B7, C5, D1, F4, G3
But he that lacketh these things is blind, and cannot see afar off, and hath forgotten that he was purged from his old sins. (2 Peter 1:_)

For D8, F2, H9
And let the maiden which pleaseth the king be queen instead of Vashti. And the thing pleased the king; and he did so. (Esther 2:_)

For G6, H8, I2
For there is one God, and one mediator between God and men, the man Christ Jesus. (1 Timothy 2:_)

	A	B	C	D	E	F	G	H	I
1									
2									
3									
4									
5									
6									
7									
8									
9									

Starter Numbers in Order:
8, 1, 3, 7, 6, 2, 9, 4, 5

PUZZLE 10
Easy

	A	B	C	D	E	F	G	H	I
1		H		M	I	S		T	O
2	E		T		H				
3	O		S	E			I		L
4	I				L			E	
5	F			S			L		H
6		L	H	I	E		S		M
7	H		L	T	O	E		S	
8		T	I	F			O		
9	S		E			I	H	F	

Hint: Column B

The victim commits _____ __ you. (Psalm 10:14 NIV)

	A	B	C	D	E	F	G	H	I
1		C		E	N	R	L	S	
2			N		L	C			R
3	L	R		U			E		N
4	C			N			I	U	
5	S	I	L		C				E
6		U		R	I			L	
7	R			L		I		E	
8	U		O		R	N	C		
9		L			U	E		N	O

Hint: Row 4

And they said, _____ the centurion, a just man, and one that feareth God. . . (Acts 10:22)

PUZZLE 12
Easy

For A2, B6, C8, D7, G9, I3
But unto the Son he saith, Thy throne, O God, is for ever and ever: a sceptre of righteousness is the scepter of thy kingdom. (Hebrews 1:_)

For A3, B7, C5, E8, I4
And they continued three years without war between Syria and Israel. (1 Kings 22:_)

For A6, D1, H4
For it is sanctified by the word of God and prayer. (1 Timothy 4:_)

For A7, E3, F5, H2
Hereby know ye the Spirit of God: Every spirit that confesseth that Jesus Christ is come in the flesh is of God. (1 John 4:_)

For B8, D9, E4, F3, G6, H7, I1
Then the king held out the golden sceptre toward Esther. So Esther arose, and stood before the king. (Esther 8:_)

For C1, E7, H3
Yet Michael the archangel, when contending with the devil he disputed about the body of Moses, durst not bring against him a railing accusation, but said, The Lord rebuke thee. (Jude _)

For C4, D3, E6, F7, G5, I8
Be careful for nothing; but in every thing by prayer and supplication with thanksgiving let your requests be made known unto God. (Philippians 4:_)

For D5, E2, F9
A prudent man foreseeth the evil, and hideth himself: but the simple pass on, and are punished. (Proverbs 22:_)

For F1, G2, I7
And the peace of God, which passeth all understanding, shall keep your hearts and minds through Christ Jesus. (Philippians 4:_)

	A	B	C	D	E	F	G	H	I
1									
2									
3									
4									
5									
6									
7									
8									
9									

Starter Numbers in Order:
8, 1, 5, 2, 4, 9, 6, 3, 7

PUZZLE 13
Easy

For A1, B7
For God hath not called us unto uncleanness, but unto holiness.
(1 Thessalonians 4:_)

For A3, D1, F4, I2
Let your speech be always with grace, seasoned with salt, that ye
may know how ye ought to answer every man. (Colossians 4:_)

For A6, D9, F2, I5
I John, who also am your brother, and companion in tribulation,
and in the kingdom and patience of Jesus Christ, was in the isle
that is called Patmos, for the word of God, and for the testimony
of Jesus Christ. (Revelation 1:_)

For A8, C6, D7, E2, F5, G4, H3
While they behold your chaste conversation coupled with fear. . .
(1 Peter 3:_)

For A9, B4, D3, E5, G8, H2
For Mordecai was great in the king's house, and his fame went out
throughout all the provinces: for this man Mordecai waxed greater
and greater. (Esther 9:_)

For B2, D5, G1, H6
But if ye be without chastisement, whereof all are partakers, then
are ye bastards, and not sons. (Hebrews 12:_)

For B3, C9, D6, E8, F1, I7
Now the end of the commandment is charity out of a pure heart,
and of a good conscience, and of faith unfeigned: (1 Timothy 1:_)

For C2, F3, G5, H8, I1
Josiah was eight years old when he began to reign, and he reigned
thirty and one years in Jerusalem. (2 Kings 22:_)

For C5, D8, H7, I4
Through wisdom is an house builded; and by understanding it is
established. (Proverbs 24:_)

	A	B	C	D	E	F	G	H	I
1									
2									
3									
4									
5									
6									
7									
8									
9									

Starter Numbers in Order:
7, 6, 9, 2, 4, 8, 5, 1, 3

PUZZLE 14
Easy

For A2, C7, E8, F1, G5, H3, I9
For if that first covenant had been faultless, then should no place
have been sought for the second. (Hebrews 8:_)

For A3, B6, C9, D5, G8, H1
And it was told Saul that David was fled to Gath: and he sought
no more again for him. (1 Samuel 27:_)

For A5, B7, D8, E3, G2, I6
Therefore let us not sleep, as do others; but let us watch and be
sober. (1 Thessalonians 5:_)

For A9, C6, D1, F8, I7
Now when Ezra had prayed, and when he had confessed, weeping
and casting himself down before the house of God. . . (Ezra 10:_)

For B1, D2, F6
To know wisdom and instruction; to perceive the words of
understanding. . . (Proverbs 1:_)

For B2, C5, G7, H4, I1
A poor man that oppresseth the poor is like a sweeping rain which
leaveth no food. (Proverbs 28:_)

For B8, E4, F9, I5
And when he had opened the fifth seal, I saw under the altar the
souls of them that were slain for the word of God, and for the
testimony which they held. (Revelation 6:_)

For C3, F5, H8, I2
Not by works of righteousness which we have done, but according
to his mercy he saved us, by the washing of regeneration, and
renewing of the Holy Ghost. (Titus 3:_)

For E7, H6
Though he were a Son, yet learned he obedience by the things
which he suffered. (Hebrews 5:_)

	A	B	C	D	E	F	G	H	I
1									
2									
3									
4									
5									
6									
7									
8									
9									

Starter Numbers in Order:
7, 4, 6, 1, 2, 3, 9, 5, 8

PUZZLE 15
Easy

For A3, B5, C8, D1, E4
Thou madest him a little lower than the angels; thou crownedst him with glory and honour, and didst set him over the works of thy hands. (Hebrews 2:_)

For A4, E9, F6, G7
Keep my commandments, and live; and my law as the apple of thine eye. (Proverbs 7:_)

For A7, B1, F8, G5, H9, I2
Who gave himself a ransom for all, to be testified in due time. . . (1 Timothy 2:_)

For B3, E2, I7
And they sung a new song, saying, Thou art worthy to take the book, and to open the seals thereof: for thou was slain, and hast redeemed us to God by thy blood. (Revelation 5:_)

For B4, D5, F2, G9
And he said unto him, Why art thou, being the king's son, lean from day to day? wilt thou not tell me? And Amnon said unto him, I love Tamar, my brother Absalom's sister. (2 Samuel 13:_)

For B7, D9, F5, I6
On that night could not the king sleep, and he commanded to bring the book of records of the chronicles; and they were read before the king. (Esther 6:_)

For B9, E6, F3, G2, I4
Let your conversation be without covetousness; and be content with such things as ye have: for he hath said, I will never leave thee, nor forsake thee. (Hebrews 13:_)

For C2, D7, F1, G4, H3, I8
Every moving thing that liveth shall be meat for you; even as the green herb have I given you all things. (Genesis 9:_)

For C9, E7, H1
Be not thou therefore ashamed of the testimony of our Lord, nor of me his prisoner: but be thou partaker of the afflictions of the gospel according to the power of God. (2 Timothy 1:_)

	A	B	C	D	E	F	G	H	I
1									
2									
3									
4									
5									
6									
7									
8									
9									

Starter Numbers in Order:
7, 2, 6, 9, 4, 1, 5, 3, 8

PUZZLE 16
Easy

	A	B	C	D	E	F	G	H	I
1			N			E	H	O	R
2	M	O		H	N				
3			H		I		M	B	
4	H				R	N	B		I
5	N	E		B					
6		Z	R		M			N	E
7	O	H	Z	R			N	I	
8	R				O	I	Z		
9			M			B			O

Hint: Column G

But the Philistines took him. . .and bound ___ with fetters
of _____/brass; and he did grind in the prison house.
(Judges 16:21)

	A	B	C	D	E	F	G	H	I
1				I		N	S		D
2	I	H	G			S		L	
3	N	D		H		K	G		
4		S			N				H
5		N		K			I		
6	G	K		S	I		O		L
7		O	L					G	K
8			N	G	H	O		D	S
9	S					D			O

Hint: Row 8

They put him in ward in chains, and brought him to the _____ of Babylon: they brought him into _____, that his voice should no more be heard upon the mountains of Israel. (Ezekiel 19:9)

PUZZLE 18
Easy

For A1, B6, C9, D4, G8, H3, I5
A double minded man is unstable in all his ways. (James 1:_)

For A2, C7, F6
And when the woman of Tekoah spake to the king, she fell on her face to the ground, and did obeisance, and said, Help, O king. (2 Samuel 14:_)

For A4, D6, E3, F9, G5
Now Benjamin begat Bela his firstborn, Ashbel the second, and Aharah the third. (1 Chronicles 8:_)

For A6, D7, G2, I4
A wise servant shall have rule over a son that causeth shame, and shall have part of the inheritance among the brethren. (Proverbs 17:_)

For A7, C6, D5, E8, F2
But let him ask in faith, nothing wavering. For he that wavereth is like a wave of the sea driven with the wind and tossed. (James 1:_)

For A8, B5, C2, F1, I7
That being justified by his grace, we should be made heirs according to the hope of eternal life. (Titus 3:_)

For B1, C4, F5, G6
If any of you lack wisdom, let him ask of God, that giveth to all men liberally, and upbraideth not; and it shall be given him. (James 1:_)

For C3, D2, F4, G7, H1, I6
And I went unto the angel, and said unto him, Give me the little book. And he said unto me, Take it, and eat it up; and it shall make thy belly bitter, but it shall be in thy mouth sweet as honey. (Revelation 10:_)

For D1, G4, H9, I2
And Sarai Abram's wife took Hagar her maid the Egyptian, after Abram had dwelt ten years in the land of Canaan, and gave her to her husband Abram to be his wife. (Genesis 16:_)

	A	B	C	D	E	F	G	H	I
1									
2									
3									
4									
5									
6									
7									
8									
9									

Starter Numbers in Order:
8, 4, 1, 2, 6, 7, 5, 9, 3

PUZZLE 19
Easy

For A4, B8, E3, G5, H7, I1
And she again bare his brother Abel. And Abel was a keeper of sheep, but Cain was a tiller of the ground. (Genesis 4:_)

For A5, C1, D7, E4, H6
A whip for the horse, a bridle for the ass, and a rod for the fool's back. . . (Proverbs 26:_)

For A8, E1, F6
But the tongue can no man tame; it is an unruly evil, full of deadly poison. (James 3:_)

For A9, B3, C5, E6, G2, I4
If any man have an ear, let him hear. (Revelation 13:_)

For B1, E7, F3, H2, I8
And beside this, giving all diligence, add to your faith virtue; and to virtue knowledge. (2 Peter 1:_)

For B6, C7, D4, F8, G3
And the king went to Gibeon to sacrifice there; for that was the great high place: a thousand burnt offerings did Solomon offer upon that altar. (1 Kings 3:_)

For B7, H9, I5
But he giveth more grace. Wherefore he saith, God resisteth the proud, but giveth grace unto the humble. (James 4:_)

For C8, D2, E9
On that day did the king Ahasuerus give the house of Haman the Jews' enemy unto Esther the queen. (Esther 8:_)

For G9, H3, I6
For we brought nothing into this world, and it is certain we can carry nothing out. (1 Timothy 6:_)

	A	B	C	D	E	F	G	H	I
1									
2									
3									
4									
5									
6									
7									
8									
9									

Starter Numbers in Order:
2, 3, 8, 9, 5, 4, 6, 1, 7

PUZZLE 20
Easy

For A1, B7, D8, E4, G5
And here is the mind which hath wisdom. The seven heads are seven mountains, on which the woman sitteth. (Revelation 17:_)

For A3, B8, C5
He removed the high places, and brake the images, and cut down the groves, and brake in pieces the brasen serpent that Moses had made. (2 Kings 18:_)

For A7, C4, D1, E8, F5, G9, H3
This then is the message which we have heard of him, and declare unto you, that God is light, and in him is no darkness at all.
(1 John 1:_)

For A9, B5, F6, H4, I8
Draw nigh to God, and he will draw nigh to you. Cleanse your hands, ye sinners; and purify your hearts, ye double minded.
(James 4:_)

For B1, D6, E3, I5
Even as Sara obeyed Abraham, calling him lord: whose daughters ye are, as long as ye do well, and are not afraid with any amazement. . . (1 Peter 3:_)

For B4, C1, E7, F3, G2, H6
Beloved, let us love one another: for love is of God; and every one that loveth is born of God, and knoweth God. (1 John 4:_)

For C2, E5, F8, G7, H1
Give ear to my words, O Lord, consider my meditation. (Psalm 5:_)

For C9, D2, H8, I1
And Abraham said of Sarah his wife, She is my sister: and Abimelech king of Gerar sent, and took Sarah. (Genesis 20:_)

For D4, E9, F1, H5
And I appeared unto Abraham, unto Isaac, and unto Jacob, by the name of God Almighty, but by my name JEHOVAH was I not known to them. (Exodus 6:_)

	A	B	C	D	E	F	G	H	I
1									
2									
3									
4									
5									
6									
7									
8									
9									

Starter Numbers in Order:
9, 4, 5, 8, 6, 7, 1, 2, 3

PUZZLE 21
Easy

For A1, C9, E3, F6, I8
For this is he that was spoken of by the prophet Esaias, saying, The voice of one crying in the wilderness, Prepare ye the way of the Lord, make his paths straight. (Matthew 3:_)

For A3, B9, C6, D1, E7, F5, G4
And men were scorched with great heat, and blasphemed the name of God, which hath power over these plagues: and they repented not to give him glory. (Revelation 16:_)

For A5, C7, D8, F1, G9, H3
And the first beast was like a lion, and the second beast like a calf, and the third beast had a face as a man, and the fourth beast was like a flying eagle. (Revelation 4:_)

For A9, B3, D4, E2, F8, G1
For Sarah conceived, and bare Abraham a son in his old age, at the set time of which God had spoken to him. (Genesis 21:_)

For B4, H2, I5
Whoso loveth instruction loveth knowledge: but he that hateth reproof is brutish. (Proverbs 12:_)

For B6, C1, H5, I9
And now I beseech thee, lady, not as though I wrote a new commandment unto thee, but that which we had from the beginning, that we love one another. (2 John _)

For B8, E6, I1
Be ye also patient; stablish your hearts: for the coming of the Lord draweth nigh. (James 5:_)

For E9
And also for the innocent blood that he shed: for he filled Jerusalem with innocent blood; which the LORD would not pardon. (2 Kings 24:_)

For G6, H7, I3
Humble yourselves therefore under the mighty hand of God, that he may exalt you in due time. (1 Peter 5:_)

	A	B	C	D	E	F	G	H	I
1									
2									
3									
4									
5									
6									
7									
8									
9									

Starter Numbers in Order:
3, 9, 7, 2, 1, 5, 8, 4, 6

Fun BIBLE **SUDOKU 2**

PUZZLE 22
Easy

	A	B	C	D	E	F	G	H	I
1	W				A	I		K	E
2		K	M	L	W		T	I	
3	T	E		K	R				
4			A		K	R	W		T
5		I		W			L		A
6	M		T					R	
7		R	A	T	K			L	W
8	L		E		I	W		T	
9		T				L	I	A	

Hint: Column A

He asked _____, and she gave him _____; she brought forth butter in a lordly dish. (Judges 5:25)

	A	B	C	D	E	F	G	H	I
1	Y	H	E	I	L	N	D	O	W
2	D	N	O	E	W	Y	L	H	I
3	W	I	L	D	H	O	N	E	Y
4	E	Y	W	N	D	H	O	I	L
5	L	D	N	O	I	W	E	Y	H
6	I	O	H	Y	E	L	W	D	N
7	H	E	I	L	N	D	Y	W	O
8	N	W	Y	H	O	E	I	L	D
9	O	L	D	W	Y	I	H	N	E

Hint: Row 3

And his meat was locusts and <u>wild honey</u>. (Matthew 3:4)

PUZZLE 24
Easy

For A2, B5, C9, D6
But if any provide not for his own, and specially for those of his
own house, he hath denied the faith, and is worse than an infidel.
(1 Timothy 5:_)

For A3, B8, D7, H6
Then shalt thou understand righteousness, and judgment, and
equity; yea, every good path. (Proverbs 2:_)

For A5, F9, G1, H7
One God and Father of all, who is above all, and through all, and
in you all. . . (Ephesians 4:_)

For A8, C2, E5, F3, G7, I1
And the chief priests accused him of many things: but he answered
nothing. (Mark 15:_)

For B1, D8, F4, H3, I7
And upon her forehead was a name written, MYSTERY,
BABYLON THE GREAT, THE MOTHER OF HARLOTS
AND ABOMINATIONS OF THE EARTH. (Revelation 17:_)

For B3, C6, E9, F2, G4, I8
Submit yourselves therefore to God. Resist the devil, and he will
flee from you. (James 4:_)

For B4, G9, H5
And Esther answered, If it seem good unto the king, let the king
and Haman come this day unto the banquet that I have prepared
for him. (Esther 5:_)

For B7, C1, D3, F6, H9, I2
To every thing there is a season, and a time to every purpose under
the heaven. (Ecclesiastes 3:_)

For C3, D1, F7, G8, H2, I5
Surely I am more brutish than any man, and have not the
understanding of a man. (Proverbs 30:_)

	A	B	C	D	E	F	G	H	I
1									
2									
3									
4									
5									
6									
7									
8									
9									

Starter Numbers in Order:
8, 9, 6, 3, 5, 7, 4, 1, 2

PUZZLE 25
Easy

For A1, D4, F9
Know ye not that we shall judge angels? how much more things
that pertain to this life? (1 Corinthians 6:_)

For A2, B5, E3
How is the gold become dim! how is the most fine gold changed!
(Lamentations 4:_)

For A4, B1, F6, G2, H5, I8
Give instruction to a wise man, and he will be yet wiser: teach a
just man, and he will increase in learning. (Proverbs 9:_)

For A6, B3, C8, D7, F1
But godliness with contentment is great gain. (1 Timothy 6:_)

For A7, C2, D1, G4, H9, I3
And the angel of the LORD appeared unto him in a flame of fire
out of the midst of a bush: and he looked, and, behold, the bush
burned with fire, and the bush was not consumed. (Exodus 3:_)

For A9, D8, F3, G7, H1
But the rest of the dead lived not again until the thousand years
were finished. This is the first resurrection. (Revelation 20:_)

For B4, C3, D5, E7, F2, H6, I1
If ye fulfil the royal law according to the scripture, Thou shalt love
thy neighbour as thyself, ye do well. (James 2:_)

For B7, C6, D9, F5, G8
Casting all your care upon him; for he careth for you. . .
(1 Peter 5:_)

For B9, H7, I6
For it is impossible for those who were once enlightened, and have
tasted of the heavenly gift, and were made partakers of the Holy
Ghost. (Hebrews 6:_)

	A	B	C	D	E	F	G	H	I
1									
2									
3									
4									
5									
6									
7									
8									
9									

Starter Numbers in Order:
3, 1, 9, 6, 2, 5, 8, 7, 4

PUZZLE 26
Easy

For A1, B8, F3, H2
To an inheritance incorruptible, and undefiled, and that fadeth not away, reserved in heaven for you. . . (1 Peter 1:_)

For A2, B5, C8, D6, F1, G4, I9
For they were departed from Rephidim, and were come to the desert of Sinai, and had pitched in the wilderness; and there Israel camped before the mount. (Exodus 19:_)

For A4, B3, C7, D5, E2, F9, G1, H6, I8
And above all things have fervent charity among yourselves: for charity shall cover the multitude of sins. (1 Peter 4:_)

For A5, C9, D3, F4, G6, H7, I1
And there was war in heaven: Michael and his angels fought against the dragon; and the dragon fought and his angels. (Revelation 12:_)

For A9, B1, C4, D8, G2
I wrote unto the church: but Diotrephes, who loveth to have the preeminence among them, receiveth us not. (3 John _)

For B6, D7, F5, H4
And in their mouth was found no guile: for they are without fault before the throne of God. (Revelation 14:_)

For C2, D1, H9, I3
The hand of the LORD was upon me, and carried me out in the spirit of the LORD, and set me down in the midst of the valley which was full of bones. (Ezekiel 37:_)

For D9, E6, H8, I5
But this thou hast, that thou hatest the deeds of the Nicolaitanes, which I also hate. (Revelation 2:_)

For F7, G8, H1
Are ye so foolish? having begun in the Spirit, are ye now made perfect by the flesh? (Galatians 3:_)

	A	B	C	D	E	F	G	H	I
1									
2									
3									
4									
5									
6									
7									
8									
9									

Starter Numbers in Order:
4, 2, 8, 7, 9, 5, 1, 6, 3

For A2, B6, D5, E8, F1, G4
Be sober, be vigilant; because your adversary the devil, as a roaring lion, walketh about, seeking whom he may devour. (1 Peter 5:_)

For A5, B7, D9, E2, H8, I3
For there are three that bear record in heaven, the Father, the Word, and the Holy Ghost: and these three are one. (1 John 5:_)

For A9, B4, G7, H6, I1
In whom are hid all the treasures of wisdom and knowledge. . . (Colossians 2:_)

For B1, C5, E7, F6, G2
Trust in the LORD with all thine heart; and lean not unto thine own understanding. (Proverbs 3:_)

For B3, C9, I5
He that is despised, and hath a servant, is better than he that honoureth himself, and lacketh bread. (Proverbs 12:_)

For B8, F3, I2
He that saith he abideth in him ought himself also so to walk, even as he walked. (1 John 2:_)

For B9, D8, E4
Come, and let us return unto the LORD: for he hath torn, and he will heal us; he hath smitten, and he will bind us up. (Hosea 6:_)

For C2, D1, G3, H4, I8
But let it be the hidden man of the heart, in that which is not corruptible, even the ornament of a meek and quiet spirit, which is in the sight of God of great price. . . (1 Peter 3:_)

For E3, F5, G9
And when they had bound him, they led him away, and delivered him to Pontius Pilate the governor. (Matthew 27:_)

	A	B	C	D	E	F	G	H	I
1									
2									
3									
4									
5									
6									
7									
8									
9									

Starter Numbers in Order:
8, 7, 3, 5, 9, 6, 1, 4, 2

PUZZLE 28
Easy

	A	B	C	D	E	F	G	H	I
1	R	G	E	O	S	I	V	I	F
2	I	S	V	R	E	F	G	U	O
3	F	O	U	V	U	G	E	S	R
4	S	V	R	E	F	U	I	O	G
5	U	I	F	G	R	O	S	E	V
6	G	E	O	S	I	V	R	F	U
7	V	U	G	I	O	S	F	R	E
8	O	R	S	F	V	E	I	G	U
9	E	F	I	U	G	R	O	V	S

Hint: Column I

And ___forgive us___ our debts, as we forgive our debtors.
(Matthew 6:12)

	A	B	C	D	E	F	G	H	I
1		A	O			F			E
2	P								A
3		R		O	I			H	P
4		P		I	F			O	
5	O	F	R		P	H		I	M
6		H	E	M	A			F	
7		E	H			I	M		
8	F			R	E				O
9			P				R		I

Hint: Row 5

The Philistines also came and spread themselves in the valley
__ _____. (2 Samuel 5:18)

PUZZLE 30
Easy

For A2, C5, G8, I4
And in those days shall men seek death, and shall not find it; and shall desire to die, and death shall flee from them. (Revelation 9:_)

For A4, F9, I8
In flaming fire taking vengeance on them that know not God, and that obey not the gospel of our Lord Jesus Christ. . .
(2 Thessalonians 1:_)

For A6, B8, C2, F7, G1
And when he was come out of the ship, immediately there met him out of the tombs a man with an unclean spirit. (Mark 5:_)

For A7, B5, E8, G4, H1
O ye simple, understand wisdom: and, ye fools, be ye of an understanding heart. (Proverbs 8:_)

For A8, C6, H5, I1
Woe is me! for I am as when they have gathered the summer fruits, as the grapegleanings of the vintage: there is no cluster to eat: my soul desired the firstripe fruit. (Micah 7:_)

For A9, D3, H2
Saying with a loud voice, Fear God, and give glory to him; for the hour of his judgment is come. . . (Revelation 14:_)

For B9, E2, I3
An hypocrite with his mouth destroyeth his neighbour: but through knowledge shall the just be delivered. (Proverbs 11:_)

For C8, D1, G2, I6
And when the chief Shepherd shall appear, ye shall receive a crown of glory that fadeth not away. (1 Peter 5:_)

For C9, D7, F3, G5, I2
For this is the will of God, even your sanctification, that ye should abstain from fornication. (1 Thessalonians 4:_)

	A	B	C	D	E	F	G	H	I
1									
2									
3									
4									
5									
6									
7									
8									
9									

Starter Numbers in Order:
6, 8, 2, 5, 1, 7, 9, 4, 3

PUZZLE 31
Easy

For A1, B4, D5, E7
But the Lord is faithful, who shall stablish you, and keep you from evil. (2 Thessalonians 3:_)

For A3, C6, I5
The light of the righteous rejoiceth: but the lamp of the wicked shall be put out. (Proverbs 13:_)

For A5, D3, E6, G9
In the seventh month, in the one and twentieth day of the month, came the word of the LORD by the prophet Haggai, saying. . . (Haggai 2:_)

For A8, C3, D4, F1, G7, H6, I2
But his father and his mother knew not that it was of the LORD, that he sought an occasion against the Philistines: for at that time the Philistines had dominion over Israel. (Judges 14:_)

For A9, B2, D8, F6, I7
And the soldiers platted a crown of thorns, and put it on his head, and they put on him a purple robe. (John 19:_)

For B6, D1, F9, G4, H8
The first angel sounded, and there followed hail and fire mingled with blood, and they were cast upon the earth: and the third part of trees was burnt up, and all green grass was burnt up. (Revelation 8:_)

For B8, C1, E3, F5, G2, H4, I9
Whom having not seen, ye love; in whom, though now ye see him not, yet believing, ye rejoice with joy unspeakable and full of glory. . . (1 Peter 1:_)

For C5, E4, H2
Get wisdom, get understanding: forget it not; neither decline from the words of my mouth. (Proverbs 4:_)

For C8, F7, G5, I1
But I speak this by permission, and not of commandment. (1 Corinthians 7:_)

	A	B	C	D	E	F	G	H	I
1									
2									
3									
4									
5									
6									
7									
8									
9									

Starter Numbers in Order:
3, 9, 1, 4, 2, 7, 8, 5, 6

PUZZLE 32
Easy

For A2, B8, E9, G7
And when the thousand years are expired, Satan shall be loosed out of his prison. (Revelation 20:_)

For A5, B3, F8
For if God spared not the angels that sinned, but cast them down to hell, and delivered them into chains of darkness, to be reserved unto judgment. . . (2 Peter 2:_)

For A6, C8, E3, G9, H1
And I saw the woman drunken with the blood of the saints, and with the blood of the martyrs of Jesus: and when I saw her, I wondered with great admiration. (Revelation 17:_)

For A7, B4, C1, E6, F2, I5
The book of the generation of Jesus Christ, the son of David, the son of Abraham. . . (Matthew 1:_)

For B1, D6, I8
Not given to wine, no striker, not greedy of filthy lucre; but patient, not a brawler, not covetous. . . (1 Timothy 3:_)

For B9, C5, D3, E8, G4, H2
He that turneth away his ear from hearing the law, even his prayer shall be abomination. (Proverbs 28:_)

For C2, D7, E1, F4, G3, H6, I9
For now we live, if ye stand fast in the Lord. (1 Thessalonians 3:_)

For C7, D4, G5, H8, I1
And God called the light Day, and darkness he called Night. And the evening and the morning were the first day. (Genesis 1:_)

For D8, F1
A devout man, and one that feared God with all his house, which gave much alms to the people, and prayed to God alway. . . (Acts 10:_)

	A	B	C	D	E	F	G	H	I
1									
2									
3									
4									
5									
6									
7									
8									
9									

Starter Numbers in Order:
7, 4, 6, 1, 3, 9, 8, 5, 2

PUZZLE 33
Easy

	A	B	C	D	E	F	G	H	I
1	S	C	I	D	O	U	M	N	E
2	U	D	N	M	C	E	S	I	O
3	O	M	E	I	N	S	D	C	U
4	D	E	M	S	I	C	U	O	N
5	N	S	C	U	E	O	I	D	M
6	I	U	O	N	D	M	C	E	S
7	E	I	S	C	U	N	O	M	D
8	M	O	D	E	S	I	N	U	C
9	C	N	U	O	M	D	E	S	I

Hint: Column H

Nicodemus saith unto him, How can a man be born when he is
old? can he enter the second time into his mother's womb, and
be born? (John 3:4)

	A	B	C	D	E	F	G	H	I
1	S	N	H	O	Y	D	R	A	U
2	Y	O	U	R	H	A	N	D	S
3	D	R	A	U	S	N	Y	H	O
4	R	A	O	Y	D	S	H	U	N
5	U	Y	N	H	A	O	D	S	R
6	H	S	D	N	R	U	A	O	Y
7	A	D	Y	S	O	R	U	N	H
8	N	H	S	A	U	Y	O	R	D
9	O	U	R	D	N	H	S	Y	A

Hint: Row 2

Thou madest him to have dominion over the works of thy/ *your hands*; thou hast put all things under his feet. (Psalm 8:6)

PUZZLE 35
Easy

For A1, B4, C9, E2
And they called unto Lot, and said unto him, Where are the men which came in to thee this night? bring them out unto us, that we may know them. (Genesis 19:_)

For A3, B9, E8, F2, H7, I1
For if these things be in you, and abound, they make you that ye shall neither be barren nor unfruitful in the knowledge of our Lord Jesus Christ. (2 Peter 1:_)

For A6, D5, F3, G4, I2
This is he that came by water and blood, even Jesus Christ; not by water only, but by water and blood. (1 John 5:_)

For A8, C6, E4, F9, H3
He that saith, I know him, and keepeth not his commandments, is a liar, and the truth is not in him. (1 John 2:_)

For A9, B3, D8, E6, H5, I7
For I determined not to know any thing among you, save Jesus Christ, and him crucified. (1 Corinthians 2:_)

For B5, D7, H1, I4
And no man in heaven, nor in earth, neither under the earth, was able to open the book, neither to look thereon. (Revelation 5:_)

For B7, D1, F5, G8
And he entered again into the synagogue; and there was a man there which had a withered hand. (Mark 3:_)

For C2, D3, G1, I9
And I heard another out of the altar say, Even so, Lord God Almighty, true and righteous are thy judgments. (Revelation 16:_)

For H6
Open thy mouth, judge righteously, and plead the cause of the poor and needy. (Proverbs 31:_)

	A	B	C	D	E	F	G	H	I
1									
2									
3									
4									
5									
6									
7									
8									
9									

Starter Numbers in Order:
5, 8, 6, 4, 2, 3, 1, 7, 9

PUZZLE 36
Easy

For A1, C6, D4, H5, I9
Ye are of God, little children, and have overcome them: because
greater is he that is in you, than he that is in the world. (1 John 4:_)

For A3, B4, G1
And the LORD said unto Cain, Where is Abel thy brother? And he
said, I know not: Am I my brother's keeper? (Genesis 4:_)

For A6, C3, D2, F9, G4, I1
I am Alpha and Omega, the beginning and the ending, saith
the Lord, which is, and which was, and which is to come, the
Almighty. (Revelation 1:_)

For A7, C1, H2, I5
In those days the multitude being very great, and having nothing
to eat, Jesus called his disciples unto him, and saith unto them. . .
(Mark 8:_)

For A9, B2, F5, G7
And Abraham said unto his young men, Abide ye here with the
ass; and I and the lad will go yonder and worship, and come again
to you. (Genesis 22:_)

For B5, D7, E4, F1, G6, I3
Bear ye one another's burdens, and so fulfil the law of Christ.
(Galatians 6:_)

For C8, G9
These have power to shut heaven, that it rain not in the days
of their prophecy: and have power over waters to turn them to
blood, and to smite the earth with all plagues, as often as they will.
(Revelation 11:_)

For D9, E3, H8
Behold, I come quickly: blessed is he that keepeth the sayings of
the prophecy of this book. (Revelation 22:_)

For E6, F8, G3, I7
The fining pot is for silver, and the furnace for gold: but the LORD
trieth the hearts. (Proverbs 17:_)

	A	B	C	D	E	F	G	H	I
1									
2									
3									
4									
5									
6									
7									
8									
9									

Starter Numbers in Order:
4, 9, 8, 1, 5, 2, 6, 7, 3

PUZZLE 37
Easy

For A3, B7, C5, D6, F8
For it is not possible that the blood of bulls and of goats should
take away sins. (Hebrews 10:_)

For A4, G6, I1
But, beloved, be not ignorant of this one thing, that one day is
with the Lord as a thousand years, and a thousand years as one
day. (2 Peter 3:_)

For A6, D9, E4, G1
These are the generations of Noah: Noah was a just man and perfect
in his generations, and Noah walked with God. (Genesis 6:_)

For A7, B4, C3, D1, E8, G5, H9
And they journeyed: and the terror of God was upon the cities
that were round about them, and they did not pursue after the
sons of Jacob. (Genesis 35:_)

For A9, C4, F1, H2, I6
And I heard as it were the voice of a great multitude, and as the voice
of many waters, and as the voice of mighty thunderings, saying,
Alleluia: for the Lord God omnipotent reigneth. (Revelation 19:_)

For B1, C9, D8, E6, F2, H3, I7
The fear of the LORD is the beginning of knowledge: but fools
despise wisdom and instruction. (Proverbs 1:_)

For B8, D3, F4, G7
Preach the word; be instant in season, out of season; reprove, rebuke,
exhort with all longsuffering and doctrine. (2 Timothy 4:_)

For D2, F9, I4
Ask ye of the LORD rain in the time of the latter rain; so the LORD
shall make bright clouds, and give them showers of rain, to every
one grass in the field. (Zechariah 10:_)

For E2, F7, H6, I3
To do justice and judgment is more acceptable to the LORD than
sacrifice. (Proverbs 21:_)

	A	B	C	D	E	F	G	H	I
1									
2									
3									
4									
5									
6									
7									
8									
9									

Starter Numbers in Order:
4, 8, 9, 5, 6, 7, 2, 1, 3

	A	B	C	D	E	F	G	H	I
1	L	T	Y	N	I	O	E	S	U
2	E	I	O	Y	U	S	T	L	N
3	S	N	U	L	E	T	O	I	Y
4	T	E	S	O	Y	N	I	U	L
5	O	Y	I	U	L	E	S	N	T
6	N	U	L	T	S	I	Y	E	O
7	U	L	E	I	O	Y	N	T	S
8	I	O	N	S	T	U	L	Y	E
9	Y	S	T	E	N	L	U	O	I

Hint: Column C

Unto thee/ ____ will I cry, O LORD my rock; be not _____ to me. (Psalm 28:1)

	A	B	C	D	E	F	G	H	I
1	J	D	U	I	A	O	H	N	L
2	O	A	N	J	L	H	I	D	U
3	H	L	I	U	N	D	J	O	A
4	U	H	A	O	I	N	L	J	D
5	N	O	D	L	U	J	A	H	I
6	I	J	L	H	D	A	O	U	N
7	L	I	O	N	J	U	D	A	H
8	A	U	J	D	H	L	N	I	O
9	D	N	H	A	O	I	U	L	J

Hint: Row 7

Weep not: behold, the LION of the tribe of Judah, the Root of David, hath prevailed to open the book. (Revelation 5:5)

PUZZLE 40
Easy

For A3, C7, D2, E8, F5
And God blessed the seventh day, and sanctified it: because that in it he had rested from all his work which God created and made. (Genesis 2:_)

For A5, D1, E9, F6, G8, I4
Many will intreat the favour of the prince: and every man is a friend to him that giveth gifts. (Proverbs 19:_)

For A7, B2, D5, G9
To speak evil of no man, to be no brawlers, but gentle, shewing all meekness unto all men. . . (Titus 3:_)

For A9, C4, D6, E7, F2, G3
I know thy works: behold, I have set before thee an open door, and no man can shut it: for thou hast a little strength, and hast kept my word, and hast not denied my name. (Revelation 3:_)

For B3, E1, G5, H9, I2
Now the feast of unleavened bread drew nigh, which is called the Passover. (Luke 22:_)

For B9, F1, I8
There went in two and two unto Noah into the ark, the male and the female, as God had commanded Noah. (Genesis 7:_)

For C1, E6, F9, G2
Now therefore, if ye will obey my voice indeed, and keep my covenant, then ye shall be a peculiar treasure unto me above all people: for all the earth is mine. (Exodus 19:_)

For C5, D9, E4, G1
And I heard another voice from heaven, saying, Come out of her, my people, that ye be not partakers of her sins, and that ye receive not of her plagues. (Revelation 18:_)

For C9, H6
Let us be glad and rejoice, and give honour to him: for the marriage of the Lamb is come, and his wife hath made herself ready. (Revelation 19:_)

	A	B	C	D	E	F	G	H	I
1									
2									
3									
4									
5									
6									
7									
8									
9									

Starter Numbers in Order:
3, 6, 2, 8, 1, 9, 5, 4, 7

PUZZLE 41
Easy

For A1, E9, H8, I6
Better is the poor that walketh in his uprightness, than he that is perverse in his ways, though he be rich. (Proverbs 28:_)

For A2, B4, E7, F3, H6
And God shall wipe away all tears from their eyes; and there shall be no more death, neither sorrow, nor crying, neither shall there be any more pain: for the former things are passed away. (Revelation 21:_)

For A3, E4, G2, I5
And Salmon begat Booz of Rachab; and Booz begat Obed of Ruth; and Obed begat Jesse. (Matthew 1:_)

For A6, B8, D7, E2, G9, H1, I4
Be not wise in thine own eyes: fear the LORD, and depart from evil. (Proverbs 3:_)

For A7, F4, H3, I8
Ye lust, and have not: ye kill, and desire to have, and cannot obtain: ye fight and war, yet ye have not, because ye ask not. (James 4:_)

For A8, B5, D6, F7
And I looked, and behold a pale horse: and his name that sat on him was Death, and Hell followed with him. (Revelation 6:_)

For A9, B3, D1, G6
Therefore is the name of it called Babel; because the LORD did there confound the language of all the earth: and from thence did the LORD scatter them abroad upon the face of all the earth. (Genesis 11:_)

For C2, G1
And the whole multitude of them arose, and led him unto Pilate. (Luke 23:_)

For C8, E6
Thou shalt have no other gods before me. (Exodus 20:_)

	A	B	C	D	E	F	G	H	I
1									
2									
3									
4									
5									
6									
7									
8									
9									

Starter Numbers in Order:
6, 4, 5, 7, 2, 8, 9, 1, 3

PUZZLE 42
Easy

For A1, E2, G6, I9
And they had hair as the hair of women, and their teeth were as the teeth of lions. (Revelation 9:_)

For A3, F5, G1
Blessed are the meek: for they shall inherit the earth. (Matthew 5:_)

For A4, B1, C8, F6, G2
Hear me now therefore, O ye children, and depart not from the words of my mouth. (Proverbs 5:_)

For A5, C7, D6, I1
In the beginning was the Word, and the Word was with God, and the Word was God. (John 1:_)

For A8, B5, F7, H2
She crieth at the gates, at the entry of the city, at the coming in at the doors. (Proverbs 8:_)

For B6, C2, E9, H8
He that walketh in his uprightness feareth the LORD: but he that is perverse in his ways despiseth him. (Proverbs 14:_)

For B9, E5, F1, H4
And they shall see his face; and his name shall be in their foreheads. (Revelation 22:_)

For D4, G5, H7
Lest I be full, and deny thee, and say, Who is the LORD? or lest I be poor, and steal, and take the name of my God in vain. . . (Proverbs 30:_)

For D8, E6, F3, G7, I4
Children's children are the crown of old men; and the glory of children are their fathers. (Proverbs 17:_)

	A	B	C	D	E	F	G	H	I
1									
2									
3									
4									
5									
6									
7									
8									
9									

Starter Numbers in Order:
8, 5, 7, 1, 3, 2, 4, 9, 6

PUZZLE 43
Easy

For A2, C5, D1, E9, F6, H7, I4
And unto the angel of the church in Smyrna write; These things saith the first and the last, which was dead, and is alive. (Revelation 2:_)

For A3, B4, C9, F7, I8
There is that maketh himself rich, yet hath nothing: there is that maketh himself poor, yet hath great riches. (Proverbs 13:_)

For A5, C2, D8, E4, F1, G7, H6
And it came to pass at the end of forty days, that Noah opened the window of the ark which he had made. (Genesis 8:_)

For A7, C3, I1
It seemed good to me also, having had perfect understanding of all things from the very first, to write unto thee in order, most excellent Theophilus. (Luke 1:_)

For A8, B1, E5, F3, G9
And he looked up, and saw the rich men casting their gifts into the treasury. (Luke 21:_)

For B7, C1, D4, F8, G5, H3
If a wise man contendeth with a foolish man, whether he rage or laugh, there is no rest. (Proverbs 29:_)

For D3, H8, I6
Every way of a man is right in his own eyes: but the LORD pondereth the hearts. (Proverbs 21:_)

For E3, I7
If thou seekest her as silver, and searchest for her as for hid treasures. . . (Proverbs 2:_)

For F9, H1
The blind receive their sight, and the lame walk, the lepers are cleansed, and the deaf hear, the dead are raised up, and the poor have the gospel preached to them. (Matthew 11:_)

	A	B	C	D	E	F	G	H	I
1									
2									
3									
4									
5									
6									
7									
8									
9									

Starter Numbers in Order:
8, 7, 6, 3, 1, 9, 2, 4, 5

PUZZLE 44
Easy

	A	B	C	D	E	F	G	H	I
1	M			H	O			A	
2		H			F	M			
3	I		F	P				H	R
4	H		R		P	O			M
5			M	I	H		O		A
6		E		M	R	F			
7	E		I			H	R	P	
8	O	A	P		I	R		M	F
9		F		O				E	

Hint: Column E

And when Joseph saw that his father laid his right hand upon the head __ _____, it displeased him. (Genesis 48:17)

	A	B	C	D	E	F	G	H	I
1	O			W	U	N	Y	S	
2	N	S				Y	U	W	R
3	U	Y	W	S					
4	S	N			G	W	I		O
5					N	S		Y	
6		G	O	Y		R		N	U
7	I		N	G	S	U			Y
8		R							I
9	Y		U				N		

Hint: Row 9

Hide me under the shadow of thy/_____ _____. (Psalm 17:8)

PUZZLE 46
Easy

For A4, C7, D3, F6, G9, I5
The fear of a king is as the roaring of a lion: whoso provoketh him to anger sinneth against his own soul. (Proverbs 20:_)

For A5, C1, I6
And when he would have put him to death, he feared the multitude, because they counted him as a prophet. (Matthew 14:_)

For A6, B2, C8, E3, F9, I1
Wisdom is the principal thing; therefore get wisdom: and with all thy getting get understanding. (Proverbs 4:_)

For A7, E4, H1
And he said unto his people, Behold, the people of the children of Israel are more and mightier than we. (Exodus 1:_)

For A8, D9, F1, H7
Verily, verily, I say unto you, He that entereth not by the door into the sheepfold, but climbeth up some other way, the same is a thief and a robber. (John 10:_)

For B5, C3, F7, I2
And there followed another angel, saying, Babylon is fallen, is fallen, that great city, because she made all nations drink of the wine of the wrath of her fornication. (Revelation 14:_)

For B8, D2, G1, H4
Whoso sheddeth man's blood, by man shall his blood be shed: for in the image of God made he man. (Genesis 9:_)

For H6, I8
And Jesus answering them said, Have ye not read so much as this, what David did, when himself was an hungred, and they which were with him? (Luke 6:_)

For F8, G5
Give not sleep to thine eyes, nor slumber to thine eyelids. (Proverbs 6:_)

	A	B	C	D	E	F	G	H	I
1									
2									
3									
4									
5									
6									
7									
8									
9									

Starter Numbers in Order:
2, 5, 7, 9, 1, 8, 6, 3, 4

PUZZLE 47
Easy

For A2, D8, E1, F6
And Moses spake so unto the children of Israel: but they hearkened not unto Moses for anguish of spirit, and for cruel bondage. (Exodus 6:_)

For A3, F2, G5, I9
But a certain man named Ananias, with Sapphira his wife, sold a possession. (Acts 5:_)

For A6, B3, D4
And he cast down the pieces of silver in the temple, and departed, and went and hanged himself. (Matthew 27:_)

For A9, B6, C1, D5, H2, I4
Wealth maketh many friends; but the poor is separated from his neighbour. (Proverbs 19:_)

For B5, C3, D9, H8
Therefore shall her plagues come in one day, death, and mourning, and famine; and she shall be utterly burned with fire: for strong is the Lord God who judgeth her. (Revelation 18:_)

For B7, E4, G8, H6, I3
Go from the presence of a foolish man, when thou perceivest not in him the lips of knowledge. (Proverbs 14:_)

For B9, E6, I7
And Joanna the wife of Chuza Herod's steward, and Susanna, and many others, which ministered unto him of their substance. . . (Luke 8:_)

For C6, E5, F7, I1
Let another man praise thee, and not thine own mouth; a stranger, and not thine own lips. (Proverbs 27:_)

For C8, E3, G6, I2
Give strong drink unto him that is ready to perish, and wine unto those that be of heavy hearts. (Proverbs 31:_)

	A	B	C	D	E	F	G	H	I
1									
2									
3									
4									
5									
6									
7									
8									
9									

Starter Numbers in Order:
9, 1, 5, 4, 8, 7, 3, 2, 6

PUZZLE 48
Easy

For A4, G1, H6, I8
And Lot went out at the door unto them, and shut the door after him. (Genesis 19:_)

For A5, B7, D6, F9, I4
The righteous considereth the cause of the poor: but the wicked regardeth not to know it. (Proverbs 29:_)

For A9, B3, G4
And the temple was filled with smoke from the glory of God, and from his power; and no man was able to enter into the temple. (Revelation 15:_)

For B1, C9, E8, F2, H7, I3
And entering into a ship of Adramyttium, we launched, meaning to sail by the coasts of Asia; one Aristarchus, a Macedonian of Thessalonica, being with us. (Acts 27:_)

For B4, C1, F5, I2
The sluggard will not plow by reason of the cold; therefore shall he beg in harvest, and have nothing. (Proverbs 20:_)

For B6, C8, D1, E4, H9, I5
And Saul, yet breathing out threatenings and slaughter against the disciples of the Lord, went unto the high priest. (Acts 9:_)

For B8, C6, F4, H5
Go your ways: behold, I send you forth as lambs among wolves. (Luke 10:_)

For C4, G7
For God doth know that in the day ye eat thereof, then your eyes shall be opened, and ye shall be as gods, knowing good and evil. (Genesis 3:_)

For D2, F8, G3, H4
And Moses spake unto Aaron, Say unto all the congregation of the children of Israel, Come near before the LORD: for he hath heard your murmurings. (Exodus 16:_)

	A	B	C	D	E	F	G	H	I
1									
2									
3									
4									
5									
6									
7									
8									
9									

Starter Numbers in Order:
6, 7, 8, 2, 4, 1, 3, 5, 9

PUZZLE 49
Easy

For A2, B8, C6, D3, F7, G5
The king by judgment establisheth the land: but he that receiveth gifts overthroweth it. (Proverbs 29:_)

For A5, D1, I4
And Esau said, I have enough, my brother; keep that thou hast unto thyself. (Genesis 33:_)

For A9, B6, D8, F4, G1, H7, I5
And the LORD God formed man of the dust of the ground, and breathed into his nostrils the breath of life; and man became a living soul. (Genesis 2:_)

For B4, C7, G2
And whoso shall receive one such little child in my name receiveth me. (Matthew 18:_)

For B9, C3, D7, H2
Give us day by day our daily bread. (Luke 11:_)

For C1, E2, H6, I3
And he took some of his brethren, even five men, and presented them unto Pharaoh. (Genesis 47:_)

For D4, H9, I1
Now about that time Herod the king stretched forth his hands to vex certain of the church. (Acts 12:_)

For D6, E7, F3, G9
And Isaac dwelt in Gerar. (Genesis 26:_)

For F6, I7
If we say that we have no sin, we deceive ourselves, and the truth is not in us. (1 John 1:_)

	A	B	C	D	E	F	G	H	I
1									
2									
3									
4									
5									
6									
7									
8									
9									

Starter Numbers in Order:
4, 9, 7, 5, 3, 2, 1, 6, 8

PUZZLE 50
Easy

	A	B	C	D	E	F	G	H	I
1			S		N		M	G	
2			I	M		R	E		
3	O		G		E	I			
4	S		E	I	R			B	M
5		R					S		
6	M		N	E		S	I		
7	E		M		B	O		I	R
8	G		B	R	I			S	
9		I		G					O

Hint: Column F

Jesus said to them, " _____ _____ of the fish you have just caught."
(John 21:10 NIV)

	A	B	C	D	E	F	G	H	I
1	A				G				Y
2		N	S	E	Y	A		P	T
3			Y				A		
4	G					T			I
5			I				T		
6		P		A				S	
7	N	E	T		S			G	
8	P				A		S		
9			A		N	G	Y	E	

Hint: Row 3

And the LORD gave the people favour in the sight of the _____.
(Exodus 11:3)

For A1, B8, C5, D2, F9, G4, I7
Wherefore the people did chide with Moses, and said, Give us water that we may drink. And Moses said unto them, Why chide ye with me? wherefore do ye tempt the LORD? (Exodus 17:_)

For A3, D5, G6
And ye know that with all my power I have served your father. (Genesis 31:_)

For A6, C9, D8, E2, I1
And Jethro rejoiced for all the goodness which the LORD had done to Israel, whom he had delivered out of the hand of the Egyptians. (Exodus 18:_)

For A9, B2, D7, G8, H6, I3
And Jacob lifted up his eyes, and looked, and, behold, Esau came, and with him four hundred men. (Genesis 33:_)

For B5, D3, G2, H9
Therefore whatsoever ye have spoken in darkness shall be heard in the light; and that which ye have spoken in the ear in closets shall be proclaimed upon the housetops. (Luke 12:_)

For B7, F6
And the serpent said unto the woman, Ye shall not surely die. (Genesis 3:_)

For E5, F8, G9
Better is a little with righteousness than great revenues without right. (Proverbs 16:_)

For E7, F1, I8
And certain of them that stood there said unto them, What do ye, loosing the colt? (Mark 11:_)

For G7, H2, I4
Go to, let us go down, and there confound their language, that they may not understand one another's speech. (Genesis 11:_)

	A	B	C	D	E	F	G	H	I
1									
2									
3									
4									
5									
6									
7									
8									
9									

Starter Numbers in Order:
2, 6, 9, 1, 3, 4, 8, 5, 7

PUZZLE 53
Easy

For A1, D7, I3
As for Saul, he made havock of the church, entering into every house, and haling men and women committed them to prison. (Acts 8:_)

For A5, F1, I6
Blessed are the peacemakers: for they shall be called the children of God. (Matthew 5:_)

For A6, B2, E9, G7, H5, I1
Forsake the foolish, and live; and go in the way of understanding. (Proverbs 9:_)

For A9, C1, D3, G5
And the ark rested in the seventh month, on the seventeenth day of the month, upon the mountains of Ararat. (Genesis 8:_)

For B3, E7, G6, I9
Where is he that is born King of the Jews? for we have seen his star in the east, and are come to worship him. (Matthew 2:_)

For B5, E2, F8, I4
And as they were afraid, and bowed down their faces to the earth, they said unto them, Why seek ye the living among the dead? (Luke 24:_)

For B6, C9, H8
And when the people complained, it displeased the LORD: and the LORD heard it; and his anger was kindled. (Numbers 11:_)

For B8, C6, E1, G3, H7
The ransom of a man's life are his riches: but the poor heareth not rebuke. (Proverbs 13:_)

For C7, E3, F9, G2
And your father hath deceived me, and changed my wages ten times; but God suffered him not to hurt me. (Genesis 31:_)

	A	B	C	D	E	F	G	H	I
1									
2									
3									
4									
5									
6									
7									
8									
9									

Starter Numbers in Order:
3, 9, 6, 4, 2, 5, 1, 8, 7

PUZZLE 54
Easy

For A3, B8, C5, D1, F7, H2, I6
As a thorn goeth up into the hand of a drunkard, so is a parable in the mouths of fools. (Proverbs 26:_)

For A5, C2, E1, F8, H7
And the sons of Jacob came out of the field when they heard it: and the men were grieved, and they were very wroth, because he had wrought folly in Israel in lying with Jacob's daughter: which thing ought not to be done. (Genesis 34:_)

For A8, B6, D7, F3, G4, H9, I2
A king that sitteth in the throne of judgment scattereth away all evil with his eyes. (Proverbs 20:_)

For B2, E7, F1, I4
And when Paul had gathered a bundle of sticks, and laid them on the fire, there came a viper out of the heat, and fastened on his hand. (Acts 28:_)

For B4, G7
Then on the third day Abraham lifted up his eyes, and saw the place afar off. (Genesis 22:_)

For B7, C3, E9, G1
The scribes and the Pharisees sit in Moses' seat. (Matthew 23:_)

For C7, E2, F9, G5, H1, I8
Now Joshua was old and stricken in years; and the LORD said unto him, Thou art old and stricken in years, and there remaineth yet very much land to be possessed. (Joshua 13:_)

For C9, F2
Jesus answered, Verily, verily, I say unto thee, Except a man be born of water and of the Spirit, he cannot enter into the kingdom of God. (John 3:_)

For G2
For when we were yet without strength, in due time Christ died for the ungodly. (Romans 5:_)

	A	B	C	D	E	F	G	H	I
1									
2									
3									
4									
5									
6									
7									
8									
9									

Starter Numbers in Order:
9, 7, 8, 3, 4, 2, 1, 5, 6

PUZZLE 55
Easy

For A1, B6, D5, I4
Behold, I will stand before thee there upon the rock in Horeb; and thou shalt smite the rock, and there shall come water out of it, that the people may drink. And Moses did so. (Exodus 17:_)

For A3, B7, D8, H9, I1
And Esau ran to meet him, and embraced him, and fell on his neck, and kissed him: and they wept. (Genesis 33:_)

For A5, B9, E4, F1, G6, H8, I3
And you, be ye fruitful, and multiply; bring forth abundantly in the earth, and multiply therein. (Genesis 9:_)

For A8, C5, F4, G2
Provide neither gold, nor silver, nor brass in your purses. (Matthew 10:_)

For B2, F7, I8
The morsel which thou has eaten shalt thou vomit up, and lose thy sweet words. (Proverbs 23:_)

For B4, C1, D3
Cry aloud, spare not, lift up thy voice like a trumpet, and shew my people their transgression, and the house of Jacob their sins. (Isaiah 58:_)

For C3, D6, E2, H4
Now Jesus loved Martha, and her sister, and Lazarus. (John 11:_)

For C8, F6, G7
Now go and smite Amalek, and utterly destroy all that they have, and spare them not; but slay both man and woman, infant and suckling, ox and sheep, camel and ass. (1 Samuel 15:_)

For F9, G3, H5
I have compassion on the multitude, because they have now been with me three days, and have nothing to eat. (Mark 8:_)

	A	B	C	D	E	F	G	H	I
1									
2									
3									
4									
5									
6									
7									
8									
9									

Starter Numbers in Order:
6, 4, 7, 9, 8, 1, 5, 3, 2

PUZZLE 56
Easy

	A	B	C	D	E	F	G	H	I
1			S	M	O				P
2	O					S		M	
3		H		P			S	I	
4			R		I			W	H
5		M		W	R		I		
6	I		W			O		R	
7	P				W	E	M	H	
8		R		O		H		S	
9	E		H		M				R

Hint: Column A

All these things will I give thee, if thou wilt fall down and _____ __. (Matthew 4:9)

	A	B	C	D	E	F	G	H	I
1		B			I				H
2	T		I			O	B	G	A
3			G	T		A			
4	L		H			I	Y	T	B
5		G				B	O		
6		Y		H		L			
7			Y	G	L		A		I
8	H	I						L	
9		O			A	T			Y

Hint: Row 9

Behold, there came up the champion, the Philistine of Gath,
_____ __ name. (1 Samuel 17:23)

For A1, B8, F4, G7, H5, I2
And he asked him, What is thy name? And he answered, saying, My name is Legion: for we are many. (Mark 5:_)

For A2, B6, G5, H9
But he answered and said, It is written, Man shall not live by bread alone, but by every word that proceedeth out of the mouth of God. (Matthew 4:_)

For A5, B7, C1, E4, F3, G2
Oh that my head were waters, and mine eyes a fountain of tears, that I might weep day and night for the slain of the daughter of my people! (Jeremiah 9:_)

For A9, B4, D2, E7, G1, I5
And Jesus said unto them, See ye not all these things? verily I say unto you, There shall not be left here one stone upon another, that shall not be thrown down. (Matthew 24:_)

For B9, C2, E5, H3
His mother saith unto the servants, Whatsoever he saith unto you, do it. (John 2:_)

For C5, D6, F9, I1
And the Philistines stood on a mountain on the one side, and Israel stood on a mountain on the other side: and there was a valley between them. (1 Samuel 17:_)

For C8, H2
Jesus Christ the same yesterday, and to day, and for ever. (Hebrews 13:_)

For C9, E8, F2
And God sent me before you to preserve you a posterity in the earth, and to save your lives by a great deliverance. (Genesis 45:_)

For D3, E9, F5, I7
And Jesse begat David the king; and David the king begat Solomon of her that had been the wife of Urias. (Matthew 1:_)

	A	B	C	D	E	F	G	H	I
1									
2									
3									
4									
5									
6									
7									
8									
9									

Starter Numbers in Order:
9, 4, 1, 2, 5, 3, 8, 7, 6

PUZZLE 59
Easy

For A1, G9, H3
Then Jesus said unto them, Take heed and beware of the leaven of the Pharisees and of the Sadducees. (Matthew 16:_)

For A6, D1, G4, H8, I3
A fool's mouth is his destruction, and his lips are the snare of his soul. (Proverbs 18:_)

For A9, H5
Moreover the spirit lifted me up, and brought me unto the east gate of the Lord's house. (Ezekiel 11:_)

For B5, C9, E6, F1, H4
Therefore said he unto them, The harvest truly is great, but the labourers are few: pray ye therefore the Lord of the harvest, that he would send forth labourers into his harvest. (Luke 10:_)

For B7, D9, F6, H2
But in vain they do worship me, teaching for doctrines the commandments of men. (Matthew 15:_)

For C2, E9, I1
But Noah found grace in the eyes of the Lord. (Genesis 6:_)

For C3, D7, E2
After that he poureth water into a bason, and began to wash the disciples' feet, and to wipe them with the towel wherewith he was girded. (John 13:_)

For C4, D6, H1
Now Samuel was dead, and all Israel had lamented him, and buried him in Ramah, even in his own city. And Saul had put away those that had familiar spirits, and the wizards, out of the land. (1 Samuel 28:_)

For D3, F7, I8
And he saith unto them, Is it lawful to do good on the sabbath days, or to do evil? to save life, or to kill? But they held their peace. (Mark 3:_)

	A	B	C	D	E	F	G	H	I
1									
2									
3									
4									
5									
6									
7									
8									
9									

Starter Numbers in Order:
6, 7, 1, 2, 9, 8, 5, 3, 4

PUZZLE 60
Easy

For A1, D7, E6, H4, I3
And, behold, there was a man named Zacchaeus, which was the chief among the publicans, and he was rich. (Luke 19:_)

For A6, B9, C3, D5, I8
The rich ruleth over the poor, and the borrower is servant to the lender. (Proverbs 22:_)

For B3, C4, E1, H9, I5
For many shall come in my name, saying, I am Christ; and shall deceive many. (Mark 13:_)

For B4, C2, E5, G3, H7
So David and his men came to the city, and, behold, it was burned with fire; and their wives, and their sons, and their daughters, were taken captives. (1 Samuel 30:_)

For B7, C5, D1, E8, H2
Now when Jesus was risen early the first day of the week, he appeared first to Mary Magdalene, out of whom he had cast seven devils. (Mark 16:_)

For C7, D4, H8, I1
Therefore Abimelech rose early in the morning, and called all his servants, and told all these things in their ears: and the men were sore afraid. (Genesis 20:_)

For C8, F9, G1
Then Jesus saith unto them, Children, have ye any meat? They answered him, No. (John 21:_)

For D9, E3, F5, H6
And forgive us our sins; for we also forgive every one that is indebted to us. And lead us not into temptation; but deliver us from evil. (Luke 11:_)

For F4, G5
Belshazzar the king made a great feast to a thousand of his lords, and drank wine before the thousand. (Daniel 5:_)

	A	B	C	D	E	F	G	H	I
1									
2									
3									
4									
5									
6									
7									
8									
9									

Starter Numbers in Order:
2, 7, 6, 3, 9, 8, 5, 4, 1

	A	B	C	D	E	F	G	H	I
1	N	U	D			S			
2	H			A				B	
3	O				H				
4		H					B		
5			F	D	N			H	O
6	B		O					F	
7					A		D	U	B
8				F		D			
9		B		O			F	N	S

Hint: Column G

And Jacob begat Joseph the _____ __ Mary, of whom was born Jesus, who is called Christ. (Matthew 1:16)

	A	B	C	D	E	F	G	H	I
1	E		F					I	
2		N	A		I	F			E
3	P		I		E	N	A		
4		R			N		F		
5	O	F		E	R			A	N
6	N		S		P		E		
7			R			O			I
8			N		S			E	A
9	S	P		I	A		R		

Hint: Row 5

The Levites. . .were recorded chief of the fathers: also the priests, to the reign __ Darius the _____. (Nehemiah 12:22)

PUZZLE 63
Easy

For A3, F7, I8
Blow ye the trumpet in Zion, and sound an alarm in my holy mountain: let all the inhabitants of the land tremble: for the day of the LORD cometh. (Joel 2:_)

For A6, C3, D1, G2, H9, I4
And the chief priests and scribes sought how they might kill him; for they feared the people. (Luke 22:_)

For A7, E5, G9, I3
And David sent and enquired after the woman. And one said, Is not this Bathsheba, the daughter of Eliam, the wife of Uriah the Hittite? (2 Samuel 11:_)

For A8, H7
When a man's ways please the LORD, he maketh even his enemies to be at peace with him. (Proverbs 16:_)

For A9, C6, E2, I1
He is not here: for he is risen, as he said. Come, see the place where the Lord lay. (Matthew 28:_)

For B2, C8, D9, F6, H5
And he ran before, and climbed up into a sycomore tree to see him: for he was to pass that way. (Luke 19:_)

For B5, C9, D3, H1, I6
For John truly baptized with water; but ye shall be baptized with the Holy Ghost not many days hence. (Acts 1:_)

For C4, E8, H3
And Abraham said, My son, God will provide himself a lamb for a burnt offering: so they went both of them together. (Genesis 22:_)

For C7, D4, E9, F3, H6, I2
When Jesus heard these things, he marvelled at him, and turned him about, and said unto the people that followed him, I say unto you, I have not found so great faith, no, not in Israel. (Luke 7:_)

	A	B	C	D	E	F	G	H	I
1									
2									
3									
4									
5									
6									
7									
8									
9									

Starter Numbers in Order:
1, 2, 3, 7, 6, 4, 5, 8, 9

PUZZLE 64
Medium

For A1, F9, I5
And they were both righteous before God, walking in all the commandments and ordinances of the Lord blameless. (Luke 1:_)

For A4, C8, E5, G9
It was that Mary which anointed the Lord with ointment, and wiped his feet with her hair, whose brother Lazarus was sick. (John 11:_)

For A7, B6, E9, G8
When Israel was a child, then I loved him, and called my son out of Egypt. (Hosea 11:_)

For B3, D4, G2
But he that denieth me before men shall be denied before the angels of God. (Luke 12:_)

For B9, D1, E7, F4, H2, I8
And said unto him, Behold, thou art old, and thy sons walk not in thy ways: now make us a king to judge us like all the nations. (1 Samuel 8:_)

For C1, F6, G3, H9
Thus dwelt Esau in mount Seir: Esau is Edom. (Genesis 36:_)

For C3, F2, G4
Excellent speech becometh not a fool: much less do lying lips a prince. (Proverbs 17:_)

For C4, I1
The baptism of John, was it from heaven, or of men? (Luke 20:_)

For C9, D3, I6
And come to the king, and speak on this manner unto him. So Joab put the words in her mouth. (2 Samuel 14:_)

	A	B	C	D	E	F	G	H	I
1									
2									
3									
4									
5									
6									
7									
8									
9									

Starter Numbers in Order:
6, 2, 1, 9, 5, 8, 7, 4, 3

PUZZLE 65
Medium

For A1, C4, E3, F7
The God of my rock; in him will I trust: he is my shield, and the horn of my salvation, my high tower, and my refuge, my saviour; thou savest me from violence. (2 Samuel 22:_)

For A6, I3
In my Father's house are many mansions: if it were not so, I would have told you. I go to prepare a place for you. (John 14:_)

For A9, C1, D8, E2, F6
For all these have of their abundance cast in unto the offerings of God: but she of her penury hath cast in all the living that she had. (Luke 21:_)

For B2, C7, H9
Scornful men bring a city into a snare: but wise men turn away wrath. (Proverbs 29:_)

For B5, H4, I9
And ye shall be unto me a kingdom of priests, and an holy nation. These are the words which thou shalt speak unto the children of Israel. (Exodus 19:_)

For B7, D2, H6, I8
And he shook off the beast into the fire, and felt no harm. (Acts 28:_)

For D1, G8, H2
Now gather thyself in troops, O daughter of troops: he hath laid siege against us: they shall smite the judge of Israel with a rod upon the cheek. (Micah 5:_)

For D4, G5, H1
But the end of all things is at hand: be ye therefore sober, and watch unto prayer. (1 Peter 4:_)

For D9, E5, F2, H7
And Jesus said unto him, This day is salvation come to this house, forsomuch as he also is a son of Abraham. (Luke 19:_)

	A	B	C	D	E	F	G	H	I
1									
2									
3									
4									
5									
6									
7									
8									
9									

Starter Numbers in Order:
3, 2, 4, 8, 6, 5, 1, 7, 9

PUZZLE 66
Medium

For A4, F3, H2
Then said Pilate to the chief priests and to the people, I find no fault in this man. (Luke 23:_)

For A7, D8, H9, I6
Open rebuke is better than secret love. (Proverbs 27:_)

For A9, B2, F1, G8
There is a lad here, which hath five barley loaves, and two small fishes: but what are they among so many? (John 6:_)

For B3, C9, D2, F7, G4, I8
Thy silver and thy gold is mine; thy wives also and thy children, even the goodliest, are mine. (1 Kings 20:_)

For B4, E2
Remember the sabbath day, to keep it holy. (Exodus 20:_)

For B6, C7, F9, G2, I5
Which was well reported of by the brethren that were at Lystra and Iconium. . . (Acts 16:_)

For C2, I1
When Pilate heard of Galilee, he asked whether the man were a Galilaean. (Luke 23:_)

For C5, D1, E9, H6
Then Jonah prayed unto the LORD his God out of the fish's belly. (Jonah 2:_)

For C6, G3
But what things were gain to me, those I counted loss for Christ. (Philippians 3:_)

	A	B	C	D	E	F	G	H	I
1									
2									
3									
4									
5									
6									
7									
8									
9									

Starter Numbers in Order:
4, 5, 9, 3, 8, 2, 6, 1, 7

PUZZLE 67
Medium

	A	B	C	D	E	F	G	H	I
1		E						W	
2	H			R		W			M
3		W	T	H	L	M		A	O
4		L		E	M		T	O	W
5					A	H			
6	M	T	R					H	
7	O	R		W			M		
8	E		A		T	O		R	
9					R	E		L	A

Hint: Column C

Then Naomi her _____ in ___ said unto her, My daughter, shall I not seek rest for thee, that it may be well with thee? (Ruth 3:1)

	A	B	C	D	E	F	G	H	I
1	B		I	N					T
2		R		M	B			N	G
3			N	E	T			L	
4	L					M	N		
5			T	G			B	E	L
6		N	R			B			M
7		E			G		M	R	I
8	I		M	R	L				
9			B		M	N		G	

Hint: Row 2

Then he called for a light, and sprang in, and came _____, and fell down before Paul and Silas. (Acts 16:29)

PUZZLE 69
Medium

For A3, C7, D4, I8
In him was life; and the life was the light of men. (John 1:_)

For A4, B2, E1, F6, H5, I9
And at that time shall Michael stand up, the great prince which standeth for the children of thy people: and there shall be a time of trouble. (Daniel 12:_)

For A6, B1, D8, F3, H7
Evil men understand not judgment: but they that seek the LORD understand all things. (Proverbs 28:_)

For B8, I4
I think myself happy, king Agrippa, because I shall answer for myself this day before thee touching all the things whereof I am accused of the Jews. (Acts 26:_)

For B9, G6
Now Jacob's well was there. Jesus therefore, being wearied with his journey, sat thus on the well: and it was about the sixth hour. (John 4:_)

For C1, E7, F5, G9, I3
Then he said, Go, borrow thee vessels abroad of all thy neighbours, even empty vessels; borrow not a few. (2 Kings 4:_)

For C3, F8, I1
He that overcometh shall inherit all things; and I will be his God, and he shall be my son. (Revelation 21:_)

For C5, E3, G2
Who hath ears to hear, let him hear. (Matthew 13:_)

For E4, G8, H2
And Joseph knew his brethren, but they knew not him. (Genesis 42:_)

	A	B	C	D	E	F	G	H	I
1									
2									
3									
4									
5									
6									
7									
8									
9									

Starter Numbers in Order:
4, 1, 5, 2, 6, 3, 7, 9, 8

PUZZLE 70
Medium

For A2, H5
And he was with her hid in the house of the LORD six years. And Athaliah did reign over the land. (2 Kings 11:_)

For A5, C3, G1, I7
This they said, tempting him, that they might have to accuse him. But Jesus stooped down, and with his finger wrote on the ground, as though he heard them not. (John 8:_)

For A8, I3
Every valley shall be filled, and every mountain and hill shall be brought low; and the crooked shall be made straight, and the rough ways shall be made smooth. (Luke 3:_)

For B2, E3, F5
Nicodemus saith unto him, How can a man be born when he is old? can he enter the second time into his mother's womb, and be born? (John 3:_)

For B5, D7, E6
And in the greatness of thine excellency thou hast overthrown them that rose up against thee: thou sentest forth thy wrath, which consumed them as stubble. (Exodus 15:_)

For B7, C4, G2
Now there arose up a new king over Egypt, which knew not Joseph. (Exodus 1:_)

For C7, E1, G5, H8
I am the door: by me if any man enter in, he shall be saved, and shall go in and out, and find pasture. (John 10:_)

For D5, F7, G9, H1
I will stand upon my watch, and set me upon the tower, and will watch to see what he will say unto me, and what I shall answer when I am reproved. (Habakkuk 2:_)

For D9, H3, I6
Ye are our epistle written in our hearts, known and read of all men. (2 Corinthians 3:_)

	A	B	C	D	E	F	G	H	I
1									
2									
3									
4									
5									
6									
7									
8									
9									

Starter Numbers in Order:
3, 6, 5, 4, 7, 8, 9, 1, 2

PUZZLE 71
Medium

For A1, H2
Gather yourselves together, yea, gather together, O nation not desired. (Zephaniah 2:_)

For A2, B5, E3, F6
Jesus saith unto him, I am the way, the truth, and the life: no man cometh unto the Father, but by me. (John 14:_)

For A5, C8, H7
But if our gospel be hid, it is hid to them that are lost. (2 Corinthians 4:_)

For A6, D3, E8, G2
Then came Amalek, and fought with Israel in Rephidim. (Exodus 17:_)

For A8, F5, I9
Receive us; we have wronged no man, we have corrupted no man, we have defrauded no man. (2 Corinthians 7:_)

For B6, E4, G5, H8, I3
And Moses went out to meet his father in law, and did obeisance, and kissed him; and they asked each other of their welfare; and they came into the tent. (Exodus 18:_)

For B7, C2, E6, F8, I5
Then David enquired of the LORD yet again. And the LORD answered him and said, Arise, go down to Keilah; for I will deliver the Philistines into thine hand. (1 Samuel 23:_)

For B8, D5, E2, H4, I1
And Simon answering said unto him, Master, we have toiled all the night, and have taken nothing: nevertheless at thy word I will let down the net. (Luke 5:_)

For D6, E9, G4
Simon Peter saith unto him, Lord, not my feet only, but also my hands and my head. (John 13:_)

	A	B	C	D	E	F	G	H	I
1	░	░	░				░	░	░
2	░	░	░				░	░	░
3	░	░	░				░	░	░
4				░	░	░			
5				░	░	░			
6				░	░	░			
7	░	░	░				░	░	░
8	░	░	░				░	░	░
9	░	░	░				░	░	░

Starter Numbers in Order:
1, 6, 3, 8, 2, 7, 4, 5, 9

PUZZLE 72
Medium

	A	B	C	D	E	F	G	H	I
1		R		S				A	D
2	S		D	N		A		R	
3		A	I				N		
4				A		D			
5		I					H	N	
6	O		U			R	S	D	
7	N		O			I	A		U
8				H			D		
9		D				U		S	

Hint: Column H

And the same John had his raiment of camel's hair, and a leathern girdle about/_____ ___ loins. (Matthew 3:4)

	A	B	C	D	E	F	G	H	I
1		I		G			T	A	
2			G		T			W	
3	A					C			E
4			E	T			R	H	
5		A			G		W		
6			R			H	E		A
7			A	C	E	W	I		
8		T	C		R			E	
9	E						C		G

Hint: Row 7

The _____ of our Lord Jesus Christ be _____ you all. Amen.
(Revelation 22:21)

PUZZLE 74
Medium

For A1, E6, F8, G7
When the chief priests therefore and officers saw him, they cried out, saying, Crucify him, crucify him. Pilate saith unto them, Take ye him, and crucify him: for I find no fault in him. (John 19:_)

For A2, B8, D6, H5, I9
And all the people answered together, and said, All that the LORD hath spoken we will do. And Moses returned the words of the people unto the LORD. (Exodus 19:_)

For A4, B2, C7, D8, H3
Blessed are the merciful: for they shall obtain mercy. (Matthew 5:_)

For A5, F6, H8
And walk in love, as Christ also hath loved us, and hath given himself for us an offering and a sacrifice to God for a sweetsmelling savour. (Ephesians 5:_)

For A9, C2, D4, I8
For as yet they knew not the scripture, that he must rise again from the dead. (John 20:_)

For B4, D1, H6, I7
Now a certain man was sick, named Lazarus, of Bethany, the town of Mary and her sister Martha. (John 11:_)

For C3, D7, E2, G1
And whosoever will not receive you, when ye go out of that city, shake off the very dust from your feet for a testimony against them. (Luke 9:_)

For D9, E4, G5, I1
Then David and the people that were with him lifted up their voice and wept, until they had no more power to weep. (1 Samuel 30:_)

For E3
For our exhortation was not of deceit, nor of uncleanness, nor in guile. (1 Thessalonians 2:_)

	A	B	C	D	E	F	G	H	I
1									
2									
3									
4									
5									
6									
7									
8									
9									

Starter Numbers in Order:
6, 8, 7, 2, 9, 1, 5, 4, 3

PUZZLE 75
Medium

For A1, D5, G6, I7
Ask, and it shall be given you; seek, and ye shall find; knock, and it shall be opened unto you. (Matthew 7:_)

For A2, E8, I9
But now the LORD my God hath given me rest on every side, so that there is neither adversary nor evil occurrent. (1 Kings 5:_)

For A6, D1, I5
And this he said to prove him: for he himself knew what he would do. (John 6:_)

For A9, B5, E7, G1, H8
And every man that hath this hope in him purifieth himself, even as he is pure. (1 John 3:_)

For B3, G2
As soon then as they were come to land, they saw a fire of coals there, and fish laid thereon, and bread. (John 21:_)

For B4, D9, F1, G3
Then Jesus six days before the passover came to Bethany, where Lazarus was, which had been dead, whom he raised from the dead. (John 12:_)

For B7, E2, F6, G9
Be watchful, and strengthen the things which remain, that are ready to die: for I have not found thy works perfect before God. (Revelation 3:_)

For B8, E6, G4, I2
And the light shineth in darkness; and the darkness comprehended it not. (John 1:_)

For H5, I3
And Israel beheld Joseph's sons, and said, Who are these? (Genesis 48:_)

	A	B	C	D	E	F	G	H	I
1									
2									
3									
4									
5									
6									
7									
8									
9									

Starter Numbers in Order:
7, 4, 6, 3, 9, 1, 2, 5, 8

PUZZLE 76
Medium

For A2, E4, I5
And when he had spoken these things, while they beheld, he was taken up; and a cloud received him out of their sight. (Acts 1:_)

For A3, C8, D9, E2, I1
And he built altars in the house of the LORD, of which the LORD said, In Jerusalem will I put my name. (2 Kings 21:_)

For B1, C5, E6, F8, G9
For every one that asketh receiveth; and he that seeketh findeth; and to him that knocketh it shall be opened. (Matthew 7:_)

For B2, G6, H3
And he opened the bottomless pit; and there arose a smoke out of the pit, as the smoke of a great furnace; and the sun and the air were darkened by reason of the smoke of the pit. (Revelation 9:_)

For B5, D6, I7
And there appeared another wonder in heaven; and behold a great red dragon, having seven heads and ten horns, and seven crowns upon his heads. (Revelation 12:_)

For B6, C7, I9
And as he went out of the temple, one of his disciples saith unto him, Master, see what manner of stones and what buildings are here! (Mark 13:_)

For B9, E7, G2
Then Peter said, Silver and gold have I none; but such as I have give I thee: In the name of Jesus Christ of Nazareth rise up and walk. (Acts 3:_)

For C2, F5, H9, I6
And Jesus saith unto him, I will come and heal him. (Matthew 8:_)

For C9, E1, I2
As long as I am in the world, I am the light of the world. (John 9:_)

	A	B	C	D	E	F	G	H	I
1									
2									
3									
4									
5									
6									
7									
8									
9									

Starter Numbers in Order:
9, 4, 8, 2, 3, 1, 6, 7, 5

PUZZLE 77
Medium

For A2, B6, E3, F9, I4
After these things Jesus shewed himself again to the disciples at the
sea of Tiberias. (John 21:_)

For A4, D1, E9, G6
But if ye had known what this meaneth, I will have mercy,
and not sacrifice, ye would not have condemned the guiltless.
(Matthew 12:_)

For A5, C3, G4
But the voice answered me again from heaven, What God hath
cleansed, that call not thou common. (Acts 11:_)

For A6, D8, H4
He lodgeth with one Simon a tanner, whose house is by the sea
side: he shall tell thee what thou oughtest to do. (Acts 10:_)

For A9, B5, G8, I6
And again they said, Alleluia. And her smoke rose up for ever and
ever. (Revelation 19:_)

For B3, I9
Thy father made our yoke grievous: now therefore make thou the
grievous service of thy father, and his heavy yoke which he put
upon us, lighter, and we will serve thee. (1 Kings 12:_)

For B4, C7, H2
Peter therefore was kept in prison: but prayer was made without
ceasing of the church unto God for him. (Acts 12:_)

For C5, D7, E2, H6
And he had in his hand a little book open: and he set his right foot
upon the sea, and his left foot on the earth. (Revelation 10:_)

For D3, G5, H9, I1
For the Son of man is Lord even of the sabbath day. (Matthew 12:_)

	A	B	C	D	E	F	G	H	I
1									
2									
3									
4									
5									
6									
7									
8									
9									

Starter Numbers in Order:
1, 7, 9, 6, 3, 4, 5, 2, 8

PUZZLE 78
Medium

	A	B	C	D	E	F	G	H	I
1			D	W	T	R		N	S
2			N		E		U		
3	E		W		N		T	A	
4			U			N			E
5	W	T	S		A	E	R		N
6				R				U	
7		E	T			A			
8	S				U	W	D	T	R
9		W	R	D					

Hint: Column D

And the rod which ___ _____ to a serpent shalt thou take in thine hand. (Exodus 7:15)

	A	B	C	D	E	F	G	H	I
1		N					I	S	
2	S	R	U	N	E				
3	I			D					R
4	D	S							
5		E			I	N		U	D
6				R	A			E	
7		I					E		
8	B			E			R		U
9			S		U	R		B	A

Hint: Row 1

It shall bruise thy head, ____ thou shalt _____ his heel.
(Genesis 3:15)

PUZZLE 80
Medium

For A1, B8, C4
But other fell into good ground, and brought forth fruit, some an hundredfold, some sixtyfold, some thirtyfold. (Matthew 13:_)

For A2, H4, I9
And afterward Moses and Aaron went in, and told Pharaoh, Thus saith the LORD God of Israel, Let my people go. (Exodus 5:_)

For A6, E1, G3
And when they had gone through the isle unto Paphos, they found a certain sorcerer, a false prophet, a Jew, whose name was Bar-jesus. (Acts 13:_)

For A9, C5, E7, F6, H8
And there shall be no more curse: but the throne of God and of the Lamb shall be in it; and his servants shall serve him. (Revelation 22:_)

For B1, C7, D2, F8
Jesus said unto him, It is written again, Thou shalt not tempt the Lord thy God. (Matthew 4:_)

For B6, D8, G4, I7
And he reasoned in the synagogue every sabbath, and persuaded the Jews and the Greeks. (Acts 18:_)

For C3, F2, H5, I1
And he was three days without sight, and neither did eat nor drink. (Acts 9:_)

For D4, I8
And I John saw the holy city, new Jerusalem, coming down from God out of heaven, prepared as a bride adorned for her husband. (Revelation 21:_)

For D5, G8, H3
And the prophet Gad said unto David, Abide not in the hold; depart, and get thee into the land of Judah. Then David departed, and came into the forest of Hareth. (1 Samuel 22:_)

	A	B	C	D	E	F	G	H	I
1									
2									
3									
4									
5									
6									
7									
8									
9									

Starter Numbers in Order:
8, 1, 6, 3, 7, 4, 9, 2, 5

Fun BIBLE SUDOKU 2

PUZZLE 81
Medium

For A3, F6, I9
And finding disciples, we tarried there seven days: who said to
Paul through the Spirit, that he should not go up to Jerusalem.
(Acts 21:_)

For A9, E8, G2
And when Paul had laid his hands upon them, the Holy Ghost came
on them; and they spake with tongues, and prophesied. (Acts 19:_)

For B1, C7, D3, F5, H4
Then Saul, (who also is called Paul,) filled with the Holy Ghost, set
his eyes on him. (Acts 13:_)

For C1, E2, H3
And Samuel died; and all the Israelites were gathered together, and
lamented him. (1 Samuel 25:_)

For C2, D8, F4, I3
And she, being before instructed of her mother, said, Give me here
John Baptist's head in a charger. (Matthew 14:_)

For C6, F7, H8
For length of days, and long life, and peace, shall they add to thee.
(Proverbs 3:_)

For C8
The heaven for height, and the earth for depth, and the heart of
kings is unsearchable. (Proverbs 25:_)

For C9, G7, I1
There cometh one mightier than I after me, the latchet of whose
shoes I am not worthy to stoop down and unloose. (Mark 1:_)

For E5, F2, I8
And David sent out ten young men, and David said unto the
young men, Get you up to Carmel, and go to Nabal, and greet
him in my name. (1 Samuel 25:_)

	A	B	C	D	E	F	G	H	I
1									
2									
3									
4									
5									
6									
7									
8									
9									

Starter Numbers in Order:
4, 6, 9, 1, 8, 2, 3, 7, 5

PUZZLE 82
Medium

For A2, B8, D4, E1, F9, G5
And they that had eaten were about four thousand: and he sent them away. (Mark 8:_)

For A6, B7, C1, D9, E3
And when Saul's son heard that Abner was dead in Hebron, his hands were feeble, and all the Israelites were troubled. (2 Samuel 4:_)

For A9, F3, I1
She standeth in the top of high places, by the way in the places of the paths. (Proverbs 8:_)

For B5, E9, G1, I7
And he called unto him the twelve, and began to send them forth by two and two; and gave them power over unclean spirits. (Mark 6:_)

For C2, D5, F1, G9
That which is born of the flesh is flesh; and that which is born of the Spirit is spirit. (John 3:_)

For C5, D8, E4, F2, I6
And it came to pass that night, that the word of the LORD came unto Nathan. (2 Samuel 7:_)

For D3, F7, H2
And Joseph said unto his brethren, I am Joseph; doth my father yet live? And his brethren could not answer him; for they were troubled at his presence. (Genesis 45:_)

For D7, E2
And when his armourbearer saw that Saul was dead, he fell likewise upon his sword, and died with him. (1 Samuel 31:_)

For F8, G4, H9
Which when Jesus perceived, he said unto them, O ye of little faith, why reason ye among yourselves, because ye have brought no bread? (Matthew 16:_)

	A	B	C	D	E	F	G	H	I
1									
2									
3									
4									
5									
6									
7									
8									
9									

Starter Numbers in Order:
9, 1, 2, 7, 6, 4, 3, 5, 8

PUZZLE 83
Medium

For A1, C7, E5, F3
But the thing displeased Samuel, when they said, Give us a king to judge us. And Samuel prayed unto the LORD. (1 Samuel 8:_)

For A6, C3, G1
When pride cometh, then cometh shame: but with the lowly is wisdom. (Proverbs 11:_)

For A7, B1, D4, I5
And into whatsoever house ye enter, first say, Peace be to this house. (Luke 10:_)

For A9, B5, E8, H4
Ye shall no more give the people straw to make brick, as heretofore: let them go and gather straw for themselves. (Exodus 5:_)

For C4, E7
I will call on the LORD, who is worthy to be praised: so shall I be saved from mine enemies. (2 Samuel 22:_)

For C8, D3, F6, G5
And the priest said, The sword of Goliath the Philistine, whom thou slewest in the valley of Elah, behold, it is here wrapped in a cloth behind the ephod. (1 Samuel 21:_)

For E1, H3, I7
The sons of Levi; Gershon, Kohath, and Merari. . . (1 Chronicles 6:_)

For E3, G9, H6, I2
He that getteth wisdom loveth his own soul: he that keepeth understanding shall find good. (Proverbs 19:_)

For E6, F9, H8
And Pharaoh said unto his brethren, What is your occupation? And they said unto Pharaoh, Thy servants are shepherds, both we, and also our fathers. (Genesis 47:_)

	A	B	C	D	E	F	G	H	I
1									
2									
3									
4									
5									
6									
7									
8									
9									

Starter Numbers in Order:
6, 2, 5, 7, 4, 9, 1, 8, 3

PUZZLE 84
Medium

	A	B	C	D	E	F	G	H	I
1		K		N				D	
2	R		H		E		K		
3				K				H	
4			N	G	O	R			H
5	G			E				I	
6		D		I			G		
7							O		K
8			I			D		R	
9	O	E		H	G				D

Hint: Column E

Now when Jesus was born in Bethlehem of Judaea in the days of
_____ the ____, behold, there came wise men from the east to
Jerusalem. (Matthew 2:1)

	A	B	C	D	E	F	G	H	I
1		H				E		I	
2	I		T		O				
3	M			I	H			U	R
4			R	E	M	O			
5				H			R		F
6	H	E		F					O
7					F				
8	O	M			T	R		E	F	U
9		T				I		R	

Hint: Row 4

There went up a smoke out of his nostrils, and _____ out of his _____ devoured. (Psalm 18:8)

PUZZLE 86
Medium

For A1, C8, F2
And Ahab had seventy sons in Samaria. (2 Kings 10:_)

For A2, B9, F1, G7, H5
And there was a cloud that overshadowed them: and a voice came out of the cloud, saying, This is my beloved Son: hear him. (Mark 9:_)

For A4, B3, G8, H6
Go and tell my servant David, Thus saith the LORD, Shalt thou build me an house for me to dwell in? (2 Samuel 7:_)

For A6, H7
And patience, experience; and experience, hope. . . (Romans 5:_)

For B5, E9, G1
When the righteous are in authority, the people rejoice: but when the wicked beareth rule, the people mourn. (Proverbs 29:_)

For B8, C6, E1, F7, H2, I9
And Saul hearkened unto the voice of Jonathan: and Saul sware, As the LORD liveth, he shall not be slain. (1 Samuel 19:_)

For C1, D3, F9, I6
And Saul said, Bring hither a burnt offering to me, and peace offerings. And he offered the burnt offering. (1 Samuel 13:_)

For C5, E3, F8, G4
I indeed have baptized you with water: but he shall baptize you with the Holy Ghost. (Mark 1:_)

For E7, G6, H1
When Herod the king had heard these things, he was troubled, and all Jerusalem with him. (Matthew 2:_)

	A	B	C	D	E	F	G	H	I
1									
2									
3									
4									
5									
6									
7									
8									
9									

Starter Numbers in Order:
1, 7, 5, 4, 2, 6, 9, 8, 3

Fun BIBLE **SUDOKU 2**

PUZZLE 87
Medium

For A1, C5, E9, F4, G6, I8
And it came to pass, when king Hezekiah heard it, that he rent his clothes, and covered himself with sackcloth, and went into the house of the LORD. (2 Kings 19:_)

For A4, C2, E3, F6, H7
And he answered and said unto them, I will also ask you one thing; and answer me. (Luke 20:_)

For A9, D6, F2, H4
And David's anger was greatly kindled against the man; and he said to Nathan, As the LORD liveth, the man that hath done this thing shall surely die. (2 Samuel 12:_)

For B2, E6, G7
Charity suffereth long, and is kind; charity envieth not; charity vaunteth not itself, is not puffed up. (1 Corinthians 13:_)

For B3, C9, E1, I2
For he said unto him, Come out of the man, thou unclean spirit. (Mark 5:_)

For B6, F8
And David was afraid of the LORD that day, and said, How shall the ark of the LORD come to me? (2 Samuel 6:_)

For B8, H1, I4
And when Jacob saw them, he said, This is God's host: and he called the name of that place Mahanaim. (Genesis 32:_)

For D5, H8
But those husbandmen said among themselves, This is the heir; come, let us kill him, and the inheritance shall be ours. (Mark 12:_)

For E7, I3
And he said unto his men, The LORD forbid that I should do this thing unto my master, the LORD's anointed, to stretch forth mine hand against him, seeing he is the anointed of the LORD. (1 Samuel 24:_)

	A	B	C	D	E	F	G	H	I
1									
2									
3									
4									
5									
6									
7									
8									
9									

Starter Numbers in Order:
1, 3, 5, 4, 8, 9, 2, 7, 6

PUZZLE 88
Medium

For A3, B9, C6, D8
And he said, Of a truth I say unto you, that this poor widow hath cast in more than they all. (Luke 21:_)

For A6, E2, F5, H3
And they had no child, because that Elisabeth was barren, and they both were now well stricken in years. (Luke 1:_)

For A8, B5, I1
Who gave himself for our sins, that he might deliver us from this present evil world, according to the will of God and our Father. . . (Galatians 1:_)

For B2, E6, F1, G3
But Uriah slept at the door of the king's house with all the servants of his lord, and went not down to his house. (2 Samuel 11:_)

For B4, F8, H2, I9
And one told Jacob, and said, Behold, thy son Joseph cometh unto thee: and Israel strengthened himself, and sat upon the bed. (Genesis 48:_)

For B7, C1, F3, I6
All these are the beginning of sorrows. (Matthew 24:_)

For C3, E5, H4
And when Saul enquired of the Lord, the Lord answered him not, neither by dreams, nor by Urim, nor by prophets. (1 Samuel 28:_)

For C8, E7, G9, I5
And, behold, I purpose to build an house unto the name of the Lord my God, as the Lord spake unto David my father. (1 Kings 5:_)

For F9, H7
Then Darius the king made a decree, and search was made in the house of the rolls, where the treasures were laid up in Babylon. (Ezra 6:_)

	A	B	C	D	E	F	G	H	I
1									
2									
3									
4									
5									
6									
7									
8									
9									

Starter Numbers in Order:
3, 7, 4, 9, 2, 8, 6, 5, 1

PUZZLE 89
Medium

	A	B	C	D	E	F	G	H	I
1		S	N	T			O		
2				V		E			S
3	E			O				R	
4		N				V	R	O	A
5	R	D		E				V	
6	V	O	A	N		R	D		E
7		V					E		R
8			O			D		S	
9	T			S	E			A	

Hint: Column B

Sun, _____ thou still upon/_____ Gibeon; and thou, Moon, in the valley of Ajalon. (Joshua 10:12)

	A	B	C	D	E	F	G	H	I
1				O				N	
2	H	O	U		A		M		I
3	R			D	M				
4			H	I					D
5	I		D	M				A	
6	A	R		U	N			I	
7	M			A		N			O
8			R			U			
9		U			I		D	H	N

Hint: Row 6

As he neared Damacus on his journey, suddenly a light from heaven flashed _____ ____. (Acts 9:3 NIV)

PUZZLE 91
Medium

For A3, C8, E7, H6
And there were in the same country shepherds abiding in the field, keeping watch over their flock by night. (Luke 2:_)

For A5, C9, E8, G7, H1
And the whole congregation of the children of Israel murmured against Moses and Aaron in the wilderness. (Exodus 16:_)

For A7, C5, D4, E3
On that day they read in the book of Moses in the audience of the people. (Nehemiah 13:_)

For B1, E5, G2, H4
For every creature of God is good, and nothing to be refused, if it be received with thanksgiving. (1 Timothy 4:_)

For B6, C1, D5, I8
For he loveth our nation, and he hath built us a synagogue.
(Luke 7:_)

For B8, F6, G9
So Saul died, and his three sons, and his armourbearer, and all his men, that same day together. (1 Samuel 31:_)

For B9, D1, G3, I5
And she brought forth her firstborn son, and wrapped him in swaddling clothes, and laid him in a manger; because there was no room for them in the inn. (Luke 2:_)

For C3, E4, F1
Wherefore hast thou despised the commandment of the LORD, to do evil in his sight? thou hast killed Uriah the Hittite with the sword, and hast taken his wife to be thy wife. (2 Samuel 12:_)

For F5, G8, H2
And this is life eternal, that they might know thee the only true God, and Jesus Christ, whom thou has sent. (John 17:_)

	A	B	C	D	E	F	G	H	I
1									
2									
3									
4									
5									
6									
7									
8									
9									

Starter Numbers in Order:
8, 2, 1, 4, 5, 6, 7, 9, 3

PUZZLE 92
Medium

For A2, E8, G4, H7
And when the queen of Sheba heard of the fame of Solomon concerning the name of the LORD, she came to prove him with hard questions. (1 Kings 10:_)

For A6, B8, D3
And some fell among thorns; and the thorns sprang up with it, and choked it. (Luke 8:_)

For A7, B3, D9, F5, G2
We accept it always, and in all places, most noble Felix, with all thankfulness. (Acts 24:_)

For A8, F1
Being made so much better than the angels, as he hath by inheritance obtained a more excellent name than they. . . (Hebrews 1:_)

For B1, D2, G6, I9
But it came to pass, when Ahab was dead, that the king of Moab rebelled against the king of Israel. (2 Kings 3:_)

For B4, D6, F8, G3, I5
And he made haste, and came down, and received him joyfully. (Luke 19:_)

For B5, G8, H4
And Absalom met the servants of David. And Absalom rode upon a mule, and the mule went under the thick boughs of a great oak, and his head caught hold of the oak. (2 Samuel 18:_)

For B7, C2, E5, G9, H1
And they took him, and killed him, and cast him out of the vineyard. (Mark 12:_)

For C4, F7, G1
And, behold, they brought to him a man sick of the palsy, lying on a bed: and Jesus seeing their faith said unto the sick of the palsy; Son, be of good cheer; thy sins be forgiven thee. (Matthew 9:_)

	A	B	C	D	E	F	G	H	I
1									
2									
3									
4									
5									
6									
7									
8									
9									

Starter Numbers in Order:
1, 7, 3, 4, 5, 6, 9, 8, 2

PUZZLE 93
Medium

For A3, D1, G2, H5
Then answered Doeg the Edomite, which was set over the servants of Saul, and said, I saw the son of Jesse coming to Nob, to Ahimelech the son of Ahitub. (1 Samuel 22:_)

For A4, D5, F7, H9
O Lord my God, in thee do I put my trust: save me from all them that persecute me, and deliver me. (Psalm 7:_)

For A6, C1, D7, G8, I3
Then Jonathan and David made a covenant, because he loved him as his own soul. (1 Samuel 18:_)

For A9, B1, E6, F8
And this I say, lest any man should beguile you with enticing words. . . (Colossians 2:_)

For B5, F9, H6
And Jesus answered and said unto him, Get thee behind me, Satan: for it is written, Thou shalt worship the Lord thy God, and him only shalt thou serve. (Luke 4:_)

For B8, C2, F1, G4, I9
He answered and said unto them, When it is evening, ye say, It will be fair weather: for the sky is red. (Matthew 16:_)

For C6, D3, G9
And the scribes and Pharisees watched him, whether he would heal on the sabbath day; that they might find an accusation against him. (Luke 6:_)

For C9, E4, I7
But Jezebel his wife came to him, and said unto him, Why is thy spirit so sad, that thou eatest no bread? (1 Kings 21:_)

For E3, F5, I1
Now when Mephibosheth, the son of Jonathan, the son of Saul, was come unto David, he fell on his face, and did reverence. (2 Samuel 9:_)

	A	B	C	D	E	F	G	H	I
1									
2									
3									
4									
5									
6									
7									
8									
9									

Starter Numbers in Order:
9, 1, 3, 4, 8, 2, 7, 5, 6

PUZZLE 94
Medium

	A	B	C	D	E	F	G	H	I
1	O		W					E	
2	V	R			O		H	W	
3	I								
4	R				V				E
5			I			P		O	
6		H		O					S
7			S		I				W
8		I	O			E	R		
9					P			S	

Hint: Column I

He said unto them, O generation of _____, ___ hath warned you to flee from the wrath to come? (Matthew 3:7)

	A	B	C	D	E	F	G	H	I
1		T	D	R	N				
2			A	H	M	D	R	T	
3									A
4		O	H					A	T
5	D		E					M	
6		M					O		D
7	T			E	R				
8	R		N		O	M		H	E
9					T		D		

Hint: Row 8

And a certain man drew a bow at a venture/_____, and smote ___ king of Israel between the joints of the harness. (2 Chronicles 18:33)

PUZZLE 96
Medium

For A1, E7, I4
And Saul eyed David from that day and forward. (1 Samuel 18:_)

For A5, C3, D6, E1
And David sent to Joab, saying, Send me Uriah the Hittite. And Joab sent Uriah to David. (2 Samuel 11:_)

For A6
Ye know that after two days is the feast of the passover, and the Son of man is betrayed to be crucified. (Matthew 26:_)

For B4, F3, G5, I1
And they set the ark of God upon a new cart, and brought it out of the house of Abinadab that was in Gibeah: and Uzzah and Ahio, the sons of Abinadab, drave the new cart. (2 Samuel 6:_)

For B7, E3, G2
But as one was felling a beam, the axe head fell into the water: and he cried, and said, Alas, master! for it was borrowed. (2 Kings 6:_)

For B8, G9
A wise son heareth his father's instruction: but a scorner heareth not rebuke. (Proverbs 13:_)

For C5, E9, I8
Now Herod the tetrarch heard of all that was done by him: and he was perplexed, because that it was said of some, that John was risen from the dead. (Luke 9:_)

For E4, F7
When Simon Peter saw it, he fell down at Jesus' knees, saying, Depart from me; for I am a sinful man, O Lord. (Luke 5:_)

For F9, H5, I7
I have no greater joy than to hear that my children walk in truth. (3 John _)

	A	B	C	D	E	F	G	H	I
1									
2									
3									
4									
5									
6									
7									
8									
9									

Starter Numbers in Order:
9, 6, 2, 3, 5, 1, 7, 8, 4

PUZZLE 97
Medium

For A1, B5, H7
Fools make a mock at sin: but among the righteous there is favour. (Proverbs 14:_)

For A2, C8, D7, I3
So the servants of king Hezekiah came to Isaiah. (2 Kings 19:_)

For A3, D2, E8, G7
But he knew their thoughts, and said to the man which had the withered hand, Rise up, and stand forth in the midst. And he arose and stood forth. (Luke 6:_)

For A6, C7
And the king said, Is there not yet any of the house of Saul, that I may shew the kindness of God unto him? And Ziba said unto the king, Jonathan hath yet a son, which is lame on his feet. (2 Samuel 9:_)

For A7
Righteous art thou, O LORD, when I plead with thee: yet let me talk with thee of thy judgments. (Jeremiah 12:_)

For A9, D5, E2, F8, G1, H4
And this taxing was first made when Cyrenius was governor of Syria. (Luke 2:_)

For B4, C1, H6, I2
I have not dwelt in any house since the time that I brought up the children of Israel out of Egypt, even to this day, but have walked in a tent and in a tabernacle. (2 Samuel 7:_)

For D1, E6, G8
But even the very hairs of your head are all numbered. Fear not therefore: ye are of more value than many sparrows. (Luke 12:_)

For G5, I9
Thou hast a few names even in Sardis which have not defiled their garments; and they shall walk with me in white: for they are worthy. (Revelation 3:_)

	A	B	C	D	E	F	G	H	I
1									
2									
3									
4									
5									
6									
7									
8									
9									

Starter Numbers in Order:
9, 5, 8, 3, 1, 2, 6, 7, 4

PUZZLE 98
Medium

For A1, E6, I2
And as soon as he knew that he belonged unto Herod's jurisdiction, he sent him to Herod, who himself also was at Jerusalem at that time. (Luke 23:_)

For A4, E8, I6
But the poor man had nothing, save one little ewe lamb, which he had bought and nourished up: and it grew up together with him, and with his children. (2 Samuel 12:_)

For A8, D6, E2, H5
In the twilight, in the evening, in the black and dark night. . . (Proverbs 7:_)

For A9, C6, F3, G5
And Solomon did evil in the sight of the LORD, and went not fully after the LORD, as did David his father. (1 Kings 11:_)

For B2, C5, H1, I8
Annas and Caiaphas being the high priests, the word of God came unto John the son of Zacharias in the wilderness. (Luke 3:_)

For B3, D5, G4
And I wept much, because no man was found worthy to open and to read the book, neither to look thereon. (Revelation 5:_)

For B6, F8, H7
Zedekiah was one and twenty years old when he began to reign, and he reigned eleven years in Jerusalem. (Jeremiah 52:_)

For B8, C2, G9, I4
Turn again, and tell Hezekiah the captain of my people, Thus saith the LORD, the God of David thy father, I have heard thy prayer, I have seen thy tears. (2 Kings 20:_)

For C4, E5, I3
And he sent Peter and John, saying, Go and prepare us the passover, that we may eat. (Luke 22:_)

	A	B	C	D	E	F	G	H	I
1									
2									
3									
4									
5									
6									
7									
8									
9									

Starter Numbers in Order:
7, 3, 9, 6, 2, 4, 1, 5, 8

PUZZLE 99
Medium

	A	B	C	D	E	F	G	H	I
1	E			R		T			A
2		M			Y	O		E	
3	R	L				B			
4			L			B		M	
5				O	R	E			Y
6	Y	T			L		O		
7			O		M		Y		
8	B				A	L			M
9		A				Y	E	R	

Hint: Column F

The first day of the week cometh Mary Magdalene _____. . .unto the sepulchre/ _____. (John 20:1; reverse word order for hint.)

	A	B	C	D	E	F	G	H	I
1	P				T	H		S	E
2			H			A	R		
3		E			O				A
4	S						Y		
5			O	R					
6	H				Y	E	P	O	S
7		S		H	A	O			Y
8		O	T				S		
9			Y	T				R	

Hint: Row 1

Do good to them that hate you, and _____ for them/_____ which despitefully use you, and persecute you. (Matthew 5:44)

PUZZLE 101
Medium

For A3, B4, I1
And king Rehoboam consulted with the old men, that stood before Solomon his father while he yet lived, and said, How do ye advise that I may answer this people? (1 Kings 12:_)

For A7, C3, E1, G4, H2, I8
Man that is born of a woman is of few days and full of trouble. (Job 14:_)

For B1, C4, F7, G9
And he built altars for all the host of heaven in the two courts of the house of the LORD. (2 Kings 21:_)

For B2, E9, H7
A man's heart deviseth his way: but the LORD directeth his steps. (Proverbs 16:_)

For B9, C6, F3
And he said unto them, When ye pray, say, Our Father which art in heaven, Hallowed be thy name. Thy kingdom come. Thy will be done, as in heaven, so in earth. (Luke 11:_)

For C7, D4, G5
And Solomon loved the LORD, walking in the statutes of David his father: only he sacrificed and burnt incense in high places. (1 Kings 3:_)

For D5, G1, I9
And shall not God avenge his own elect, which cry day and night unto him, though he bear long with them? (Luke 18:_)

For D6, I4
And Jesus said unto them, Neither tell I you by what authority I do these things. (Luke 20:_)

For I7
Have ye suffered so many things in vain? if it be yet in vain. (Galatians 3:_)

	A	B	C	D	E	F	G	H	I
1									
2									
3									
4									
5									
6									
7									
8									
9									

Starter Numbers in Order:
6, 1, 5, 9, 2, 3, 7, 8, 4

PUZZLE 102
Medium

For A3, B5, H6, I8
And there was war between Rehoboam and Jeroboam all the days of his life. (1 Kings 15:_)

For A4, B1, H8
Then the twelve called the multitude of the disciples unto them, and said, It is not reason that we should leave the word of God, and serve tables. (Acts 6:_)

For A9, B3, E1
Moreover take thou up a lamentation for the princes of Israel. (Ezekiel 19:_)

For B2, H9, I4
And Ahab called Obadiah, which was the governor of his house. (Now Obadiah feared the LORD greatly.) (1 Kings 18:_)

For B7, E2, F6
The Son of man must be delivered into the hands of sinful men, and be crucified, and the third day rise again. (Luke 24:_)

For B8, D2, E4, H3
But Jesus yet answered nothing; so that Pilate marvelled. (Mark 15:_)

For C8, E5, F9, H1
He also that is slothful in his work is brother to him that is a great waster. (Proverbs 18:_)

For D5, E8, I2
And I heard the number of them which were sealed: and there were sealed an hundred and forty and four thousand of all the tribes of the children of Israel. (Revelation 7:_)

For E7, G3, I9
And a very great multitude spread their garments in the way; others cut down branches from the trees, and strawed them in the way. (Matthew 21:_)

	A	B	C	D	E	F	G	H	I
1									
2									
3									
4									
5									
6									
7									
8									
9									

Starter Numbers in Order:
6, 2, 1, 3, 7, 5, 9, 4, 8

PUZZLE 103
Medium

For A2, E5, F1
And the ravens brought him bread and flesh in the morning,
and bread and flesh in the evening; and he drank of the brook.
(1 Kings 17:_)

For A4, B9, F3, H2, I5
And when he saw that, he arose, and went for his life, and came to
Beersheba, which belongeth to Judah, and left his servant there. (1
Kings 19:_)

For B1, D3, F8, G5
And when the seven thunders had uttered their voices, I was about
to write: and I heard a voice from heaven saying unto me, Seal up
those things which the seven thunders uttered, and write them
not. (Revelation 10:_)

For B3, C9, E8
And go quickly, and tell his disciples that he is risen from the dead;
and, behold, he goeth before you into Galilee; there shall ye see
him: lo, I have told you. (Matthew 28:_)

For B6, H7
Who can say, I have made my heart clean, I am pure from my sin?
(Proverbs 20:_)

For C6, D1, E4, F7, I9
And he killed James the brother of John with the sword. (Acts 12:_)

For C7, F2, G6
And hired counsellors against them, to frustrate their purpose, all
the days of Cyrus king of Persia, even until the reign of Darius
king of Persia. . . (Ezra 4:_)

For D9, G2, I7
One of his disciples, Andrew, Simon Peter's brother, saith unto
him. . . (John 6:_)

For F9, G1
But it displeased Jonah exceedingly, and he was very angry.
(Jonah 4:_)

	A	B	C	D	E	F	G	H	I
1									
2									
3									
4									
5									
6									
7									
8									
9									

Starter Numbers in Order:
6, 3, 4, 7, 9, 2, 5, 8, 1

	A	B	C	D	E	F	G	H	I
1	T				A				
2	O		H	F			I	R	A
3						V			
4		W	I				H	O	
5	A		V				F	I	
6		T	O				A		
7			W			R			H
8								W	F
9	V	A			H	O			

Hint: Column G

For surely, O Lord, you bless the righteous; you surround them
_____ your _____ as with a shield. (Psalm 5:12 NIV)

	A	B	C	D	E	F	G	H	I
1	T							F	
2		S	E			R			H
3	A			F	V		S		
4							R		
5	O	F		A				S	
6			S	T	E				V
7		T				H			
8	H						V	O	A
9			V	R					E

Hint: Row 5

And they came to Bethlehem in the beginning __ barley _____.
(Ruth 1:22)

PUZZLE 106
Medium

For A1, B7, D5, E2, G6
A virtuous woman is a crown to her husband: but she that maketh ashamed is as rottenness in his bones. (Proverbs 12:_)

For A6, F8, H5
And it came to pass, when the vessels were full, that she said unto her son, Bring me yet a vessel. And he said unto her, There is not a vessel more. And the oil stayed. (2 Kings 4:_)

For A9, C3, G7
Then arose Ezra, and made the chief priests, the Levites, and all Israel, to swear that they should do according to this word. And they sware. (Ezra 10:_)

For B6, I9
The world cannot hate you; but me it hateth, because I testify of it, that the works thereof are evil. (John 7:_)

For C2, D9, F4, G8
Then take the box of oil, and pour it on his head, and say, Thus saith the LORD, I have anointed thee king over Israel. Then open the door, and flee, and tarry not. (2 Kings 9:_)

For C7, F1, G2, I4
Jesus saith unto him, Rise, take up thy bed, and walk. (John 5:_)

For C8, F5, H7
As they ministered to the Lord, and fasted, the Holy Ghost said, Separate me Barnabas and Saul for the work whereunto I have called them. (Acts 13:_)

For E1, H3
When they had heard the king, they departed; and, lo, the star, which they saw in the east, went before them, till it came and stood over where the young child was. (Matthew 2:_)

For F6, H4, I2
Nebuchadnezzar the king made an image of gold. . .he set it up in the plain of Dura, in the province of Babylon. (Daniel 3:_)

	A	B	C	D	E	F	G	H	I
1									
2									
3									
4									
5									
6									
7									
8									
9									

Starter Numbers in Order:
4, 6, 5, 7, 3, 8, 2, 9, 1

PUZZLE 107
Medium

For A1, D2, E9, I8
But the high places were not taken away: the people still sacrificed and burnt incense in the high places. (2 Kings 12:_)

For A3, B6
For, behold, the day cometh, that shall burn as an oven; and all the proud, yea, and all that do wickedly, shall be stubble. (Malachi 4:_)

For A8, B5, G9, H6, I2
And he shall restore the lamb fourfold, because he did this thing, and because he had no pity. (2 Samuel 12:_)

For A9, C4, D8, E5, F2, G1
Unto Timothy, my own son in the faith: Grace, mercy, and peace, from God our Father and Jesus Christ our Lord. (1 Timothy 1:_)

For B1, D6, E8
Riches profit not in the day of wrath: but righteousness delivereth from death. (Proverbs 11:_)

For C3, G6, H9
The way of the wicked is an abomination unto the LORD: but he loveth him that followeth after righteousness. (Proverbs 15:_)

For C8, E1, G7
So when they continued asking him, he lifted up himself, and said unto them, He that is without sin among you, let him first cast a stone at her. (John 8:_)

For G3, I5
And also let the golden and silver vessels of the house of God, which Nebuchadnezzar took forth out of the temple which is at Jerusalem, and brought unto Babylon, be restored. (Ezra 6:_)

For G4, H1
But ye shall receive power, after that the Holy Ghost is come upon you: and ye shall be witnesses unto me both in Jerusalem, and in all Judaea, and in Samaria, and unto the uttermost part of the earth. (Acts 1:_)

	A	B	C	D	E	F	G	H	I
1									
2									
3									
4									
5									
6									
7									
8									
9									

Starter Numbers in Order:
3, 1, 6, 2, 4, 9, 7, 5, 8

For A3, B9, F1
The words of a man's mouth are as deep waters, and the wellspring of wisdom as a flowing brook. (Proverbs 18:_)

For A4, C2, G9, I6
And a vision appeared to Paul in the night; There stood a man of Macedonia, and prayed him, saying, Come over into Macedonia, and help us. (Acts 16:_)

For A6, D8, I3
For the LORD had made the host of the Syrians to hear a noise of chariots, and a noise of horses, even the noise of a great host. (2 Kings 7:_)

For B4, C9, D2, E7, G3, H6
Mercy unto you, and peace, and love, be multiplied. (Jude _)

For B6, I9
And I said unto the king, If it please the king, and if thy servant have found favour in thy sight, that thou wouldest send me unto Judah, unto the city of my fathers' sepulchres, that I may build it. (Nehemiah 2:_)

For B8, C1, F3, G6, I7
And the anger of the LORD was kindled against Israel, and he delivered them into the hand of Hazael king of Syria, and into the hand of Benhadad the son of Hazael, all their days. (2 Kings 13:_)

For C4, D9, E3, I5
And now, O ye priests, this commandment is for you. (Malachi 2:_)

For D1, E8, H5
Go, wash in the pool of Siloam, (which is by interpretation, Sent.) He went his way therefore, and washed, and came seeing. (John 9:_)

For F9, H4, I1
And he leaping up stood, and walked, and entered with them into the temple, walking, and leaping, and praising God. (Acts 3:_)

	A	B	C	D	E	F	G	H	I
1									
2									
3									
4									
5									
6									
7									
8									
9									

Starter Numbers in Order:
4, 9, 6, 2, 5, 3, 1, 7, 8

PUZZLE 109
Medium

	A	B	C	D	E	F	G	H	I
1	A				T		E	H	
2				H		D			
3	D		T				L		
4	L			U		H		D	
5	E			L	O		T		
6			O	S					E
7		U			L			A	
8	O			A			D	E	
9	H					S		O	

Hint: Column D

There is nothing better for a man, than that he _____ ___ and drink. (Ecclesiastes 2:24)

	A	B	C	D	E	F	G	H	I
1				T					Y
2		G			I		N	W	
3		R	Y			A			
4	Y		N	I		H	W		
5		W	R						T
6			A		T		R		
7	W							Y	
8			I	G				N	
9	A			R			I		H

Hint: Row 9

Whosoever is _____ ___ his brother without a cause shall be in danger of the judgment. (Matthew 5:22)

PUZZLE 111
Medium

For A2, D1, G7
Then the king Ahasuerus answered and said unto Esther the queen, Who is he, and where is he, that durst presume in his heart to do so? (Esther 7:_)

For A3, D9, G8, H1
Then spake the Lord to Paul in the night by a vision, Be not afraid, but speak, and hold not thy peace. (Acts 18:_)

For A4, F2
And the man of God said, Where fell it? And he shewed him the place. And he cut down a stick, and cast it in thither; and the iron did swim. (2 Kings 6:_)

For A5, B9, H7, I6
And it came to pass afterward, that he went throughout every city and village, preaching and shewing the glad tidings of the kingdom of God: and the twelve were with him. (Luke 8:_)

For A7, B1, C4, D8, G9, I2
And he laid hold on the dragon, that old serpent, which is the Devil, and Satan, and bound him a thousand years. (Revelation 20:_)

For A9, F6, G3
Answer not a fool according to his folly, lest thou also be like unto him. (Proverbs 26:_)

For B2, D4, G6, I7
And Stephen, full of faith and power, did great wonders and miracles among the people. (Acts 6:_)

For C1, G4
The impotent man answered him, Sir, I have no man, when the water is troubled, to put me into the pool: but while I am coming, another steppeth down before me. (John 5:_)

For C7, G2
And it came to pass at the seven years' end, that the woman returned out of the land of the Philistines: and she went forth to cry unto the king for her house and for her land. (2 Kings 8:_)

	A	B	C	D	E	F	G	H	I
1									
2									
3									
4									
5									
6									
7									
8									
9									

Starter Numbers in Order:
5, 9, 6, 1, 2, 4, 8, 7, 3

PUZZLE 112
Medium

For A3, E8, G7, H6
Come, eat of my bread, and drink of the wine which I have
mingled. (Proverbs 9:_)

For A6, I2
And there were many lights in the upper chamber, where they
were gathered together. (Acts 20:_)

For A7, B1, D4, I5
Wrath is cruel, and anger is outrageous; but who is able to stand
before envy? (Proverbs 27:_)

For A9, C4, D1, F8
And the word of God increased; and the number of the disciples
multiplied in Jerusalem greatly; and a great company of the priests
were obedient to the faith. (Acts 6:_)

For C8, D3, H1
Giving no offence in any thing, that the ministry be not blamed.
(2 Corinthians 6:_)

For D7
Let not your heart be troubled: ye believe in God, believe also in
me. (John 14:_)

For E3, I4
So Haman came in. And the king said unto him, What shall be done
unto the man whom the king delighteth to honour? (Esther 6:_)

For E4, H2, I8
The rich and poor meet together: the Lord is the maker of them
all. (Proverbs 22:_)

For E6, I9
And there sat in a window a certain young man named Eutychus,
being fallen into a deep sleep: and as Paul was long preaching, he
sunk down with sleep, and fell down from the third loft, and was
taken up dead. (Acts 20:_)

	A	B	C	D	E	F	G	H	I
1									
2									
3									
4									
5									
6									
7									
8									
9									

Starter Numbers in Order:
5, 8, 4, 7, 3, 1, 6, 2, 9

PUZZLE 113
Medium

For A2, E5, F3
They that forsake the law praise the wicked: but such as keep the law contend with them. (Proverbs 28:_)

For A4, F5
All that ever came before me are thieves and robbers: but the sheep did not hear them. (John 10:_)

For A7, B2, E8, I6
A faithful witness will not lie: but a false witness will utter lies. (Proverbs 14:_)

For A9, D1, E6, G4, H8
Now before the feast of the passover, when Jesus knew that his hour was come that he should depart out of this world unto the Father. . . (John 13:_)

For B3, D6, G7
And they were all amazed and marvelled, saying one to another, Behold, are not all these which speak Galilaeans? (Acts 2:_)

For B6, C8, E7, G2, I9
And put a knife to thy throat, if thou be a man given to appetite. (Proverbs 23:_)

For C2, F6, I1
Through faith we understand that the worlds were framed by the word of God, so that things which are seen were not made of things which do appear. (Hebrews 11:_)

For C7, F2, H3, I5
And Esther said, The adversary and enemy is this wicked Haman. Then Haman was afraid before the king and the queen. (Esther 7:_)

For D4, G3, I7
The Lord is not slack concerning his promise, as some men count slackness; but is longsuffering to us-ward, not willing that any should perish, but that all should come to repentance. (2 Peter 3:_)

	A	B	C	D	E	F	G	H	I
1									
2									
3									
4									
5									
6									
7									
8									
9									

Starter Numbers in Order:
4, 8, 5, 1, 7, 2, 3, 6, 9

PUZZLE 114
Medium

	A	B	C	D	E	F	G	H	I
1	M						N	R	
2			N		R	T	A		
3			T			C			
4				T	S			A	
5	H	N		E	A		C		M
6	A		R	C		M		E	
7				M				H	A
8			H			E			S
9	S	C		R					

Hint: Column A

Haran, and Canneh, and Eden, the _____ of Sheba, Asshur, and Chilmad, were thy merchants. (Ezekiel 27:23)

	A	B	C	D	E	F	G	H	I
1	S				T				H
2			M	H			T		
3		H	E	R		M		N	
4	M			O					
5		T			S		M	E	A
6	N		S	A					R
7			N						M
8	R				A	N		H	
9	E			T		O	S		

Hint: Row 3

If we let him thus alone, all men will believe on him: and ___
_____ shall come and take away both our place and nation.
(John 11:48)

PUZZLE 116
Medium

For A1, G9
Then said Jesus unto them again, Verily, verily, I say unto you,
I am the door of the sheep. (John 10:_)

For A6, D1, E9, I5
The thoughts of the diligent tend only to plenteousness; but of
every one that is hasty only to want. (Proverbs 21:_)

For A8, E7, F3
Labour not to be rich: cease from thine own wisdom. (Proverbs 23:_)

For B4, F8, G1
It is the glory of God to conceal a thing: but the honour of kings is
to search out a matter. (Proverbs 25:_)

For B6, C2, F9
And he brought out the grove from the house of the LORD,
without Jerusalem, unto the brook Kidron, and burned it at the
brook Kidron, and stamped it small to powder. (2 Kings 23:_)

For B9, E1, H6, I3
And the same man had four daughters, virgins, which did
prophesy. (Acts 21:_)

For C3, E4
And, hardly passing it, came unto a place which is called The fair
havens; nigh whereunto was the city of Lasea. . . (Acts 27:_)

For C7, E3, F6, G5, H2, I8
In the end of the sabbath, as it began to dawn toward the first day
of the week, came Mary Magdalene and the other Mary to see the
sepulchre. (Matthew 28:_)

For G7
Blessed is he that readeth, and they that hear the words of this
prophecy, and keep those things which are written therein: for the
time is at hand. (Revelation 1:_)

	A	B	C	D	E	F	G	H	I
1									
2									
3									
4									
5									
6									
7									
8									
9									

Starter Numbers in Order:
7, 5, 4, 2, 6, 9, 8, 1, 3

PUZZLE 117
Medium

For A2, B8, D6, H7
A fool despiseth his father's instruction: but he that regardeth reproof is prudent. (Proverbs 15:_)

For A6, B9, C3, E5, F8
Hurt not the earth, neither the sea, nor the trees, till we have sealed the servants of our God in their foreheads. (Revelation 7:_)

For B4, E7, F1
Woe to the bloody city! it is all full of lies and robbery; the prey departeth not. (Nahum 3:_)

For B7, C5, F4
And I heard a voice saying unto me, Arise, Peter; slay and eat. (Acts 11:_)

For C6, D4, G9
And the LORD called Samuel again the third time. And he arose and went to Eli, and said, Here am I; for thou didst call me. And Eli perceived that the LORD had called the child. (1 Samuel 3:_)

For C7, H5
It is not for kings, O Lemuel, it is not for kings to drink wine; nor for princes strong drink. (Proverbs 31:_)

For D1, F5, G3, I7
And in Shushan the palace the Jews slew and destroyed five hundred men. (Esther 9:_)

For F2, G8, H6
As the bird by wandering, as the swallow by flying, so the curse causeless shall not come. (Proverbs 26:_)

For I2
Therefore Eli said unto Samuel, Go, lie down: and it shall be, if he call thee, that thou shalt say, Speak, LORD; for thy servant heareth. So Samuel went and lay down in his place. (1 Samuel 3:_)

	A	B	C	D	E	F	G	H	I
1									
2									
3									
4									
5									
6									
7									
8									
9									

Starter Numbers in Order:
5, 3, 1, 7, 8, 4, 6, 2, 9

PUZZLE 118
Medium

For A2
And there came out of the smoke locusts upon the earth: and unto them was given power, as the scorpions of the earth have power. (Revelation 9:_)

For A3, E2, G9
Speak not in the ears of a fool: for he will despise the wisdom of thy words. (Proverbs 23:_)

For A6, D9, F4, G1
This Ezra went up from Babylon; and he was a ready scribe in the law of Moses, which the LORD God of Israel had given: and the king granted him all his request. (Ezra 7:_)

For A7, F6, G2, I4
And the children of Israel said to Samuel, Cease not to cry unto the LORD our God for us, that he will save us out of the hand of the Philistines. (1 Samuel 7:_)

For B3, H1, I9
Every word of God is pure: he is a shield unto them that put their trust in him. (Proverbs 30:_)

For B7, C3, D5, F9, G6
And Abram was very rich in cattle, in silver, and in gold. (Genesis 13:_)

For B9, E7, G8
Now Samuel did not yet know the LORD, neither was the word of the LORD yet revealed unto him. (1 Samuel 3:_)

For C5, D2, H3
An high look, and a proud heart, and the plowing of the wicked, is sin. (Proverbs 21:_)

For C9, E5, F3, H7
I lifted up mine eyes again, and looked, and behold a man with a measuring line in his hand. (Zechariah 2:_)

	A	B	C	D	E	F	G	H	I
1									
2									
3									
4									
5									
6									
7									
8									
9									

Starter Numbers in Order:
3, 9, 6, 8, 5, 2, 7, 4, 1

PUZZLE 119
Medium

	A	B	C	D	E	F	G	H	I
1			U	R					W
2	N					W	I		D
3			D			F		U	
4					F	N	U		S
5	R	U		I	S				
6								I	N
7	W		S		I				O
8		R					F		
9	F					O		S	

Hint: Column H

And after these things I saw four angels standing on the four corners of the earth, holding the ____ _____ of the earth. (Revelation 7:1)

	A	B	C	D	E	F	G	H	I
1	P	E			O				H
2	H		S		P		W		
3			W	S			R		
4			I				H	W	
5	E	H				W			
6			S			I	P		D
7		W	O				E		P
8	I				R	P	D		
9					W			S	

Hint: Row 6

On coming to the house, they saw the child with his mother Mary, and they bowed down and _____ him. (Matthew 2:11 NIV)

PUZZLE 121
Medium

For A1, C6, H2, I7
And the king said unto me, (the queen also sitting by him,) For how long shall thy journey be? and when wilt thou return? So it pleased the king to send me; and I set him a time. (Nehemiah 2:_)

For A3, B4, E7, G1, I5
Bind them upon thy fingers, write them upon the table of thine heart. (Proverbs 7:_)

For A6, B7, C3, G8
But the Lord said unto Samuel, Look not on his countenance, or on the height of his stature; because I have refused him: for the Lord seeth not as man seeth; for man looketh on the outward appearance, but the Lord looketh on the heart. (1 Samuel 16:_)

For A8, E5, I3
But ye are a chosen generation, a royal priesthood, an holy nation, a peculiar people; that ye should shew forth the praises of him who hath called you out of darkness into his marvellous light. (1 Peter 2:_)

For A9, C2, E4
And he lift up his eyes and looked, and, lo, three men stood by him: and when he saw them, he ran to meet them from the tent door, and bowed himself toward the ground. (Genesis 18:_)

For B6, E1, G4
A man that flattereth his neighbour spreadeth a net for his feet. (Proverbs 29:_)

For B8, I6
And he tarried seven days, according to the set time that Samuel had appointed: but Samuel came not to Gilgal; and the people were scattered from him. (1 Samuel 13:_)

For D8, E6, G9, I2
But Solomon was building his own house thirteen years, and he finished all his house. (1 Kings 7:_)

For E9, F2, H5
And when his brethren saw that their father loved him more than all his brethren, they hated him, and could not speak peaceably unto him. (Genesis 37:_)

	A	B	C	D	E	F	G	H	I
1									
2									
3									
4									
5									
6									
7									
8									
9									

Starter Numbers in Order:
6, 3, 7, 9, 2, 5, 8, 1, 4

PUZZLE 122
Medium

For A2, D7, E3, I5
And Joseph commanded his servants the physicians to embalm his father: and the physicians embalmed Israel. (Genesis 50:_)

For A7, B4, F3, I8
So built we the wall; and all the wall was joined together unto the half thereof: for the people had a mind to work. (Nehemiah 4:_)

For B5, E7, G4, I1
And he could there do no mighty work, save that he laid his hands upon a few sick folk, and healed them. (Mark 6:_)

For B6, D8, H4
In the mouth of the foolish is a rod of pride: but the lips of the wise shall preserve them. (Proverbs 14:_)

For B9, E8
And he took Agag the king of the Amalekites alive, and utterly destroyed all the people with the edge of the sword. (1 Samuel 15:_)

For C2, D1
Receiving the end of your faith, even the salvation of your souls. . . (1 Peter 1:_)

For C8, D9, E1, G7
And the women answered one another as they played, and said, Saul hath slain his thousands, and David his ten thousands. (1 Samuel 18:_)

For D3, I2
Pharaoh's chariots and his host hath he cast into the sea: his chosen captains also are drowned in the Red sea. (Exodus 15:_)

For G9
Then all the people of Judah took Uzziah, who was sixteen years old, and made him king in the room of his father Amaziah. (2 Chronicles 26:_)

	A	B	C	D	E	F	G	H	I
1									
2									
3									
4									
5									
6									
7									
8									
9									

Starter Numbers in Order:
2, 6, 5, 3, 8, 9, 7, 4, 1

Fun BIBLE **SUDOKU 2**

For A3, G9, I1
For the lips of a strange woman drop as an honeycomb, and her mouth is smoother than oil. (Proverbs 5:_)

For A5, B2, I9
Now a certain man of the servants of Saul was there that day, detained before the LORD; and his name was Doeg, an Edomite, the chiefest of the herdmen that belonged to Saul. (1 Samuel 21:_)

For A6, B9, E7, H3
Who shall be punished with everlasting destruction from the presence of the Lord, and from the glory of his power. . . (2 Thessalonians 1:_)

For A9, G3, I4
For his disciples were gone away unto the city to buy meat. (John 4:_)

For B1, C7
He trusted in the LORD God of Israel; so that after him was none like him among all the kings of Judah, nor any that were before him. (2 Kings 18:_)

For B3, D9, F4, G6
And Pharaoh said, Who is the LORD, that I should obey his voice to let Israel go? I know not the LORD, neither will I let Israel go. (Exodus 5:_)

For B6, E4, F9
And the same John had his raiment of camel's hair, and a leathern girdle about his loins; and his meat was locusts and wild honey. (Matthew 3:_)

For D2, E5, G4
My soul is weary of my life; I will leave my complaint upon myself; I will speak in the bitterness of my soul. (Job 10:_)

For E3, G7, H1
And in the reign of Ahasuerus, in the beginning of his reign, wrote they unto him an accusation against the inhabitants of Judah and Jerusalem. (Ezra 4:_)

	A	B	C	D	E	F	G	H	I
1									
2									
3									
4									
5									
6									
7									
8									
9									

Starter Numbers in Order:
3, 7, 9, 8, 5, 2, 4, 1, 6

PUZZLE 124
Medium

	A	B	C	D	E	F	G	H	I
1	A	S			I	O			
2		O							
3		I	D	E		P		R	
4			I	O					
5	O	R				A	P	E	
6								I	
7		Y				I	D	S	
8				P					
9				R		E	A		I

Hint: Column B

Then the king said unto me, For what dost thou make request?
__ _ _____ to the God of heaven. (Nehemiah 2:4)

	A	B	C	D	E	F	G	H	I
1	S		A						
2		R		S	D				I
3			U	A					
4			D						
5			I			A	S		U
6	T			R				D	H
7		A						H	E
8	I								D
9		T		E	R				A

Hint: Row 7

They sent a letter unto him, wherein was written thus; Unto _____ ___ king, all peace. (Ezra 5:7)

PUZZLE 126
Medium

For A1, C4, G5, I9
And Ezra blessed the Lord, the great God. And all the people answered, Amen, Amen, with lifting up their hands: and they bowed their heads, and worshipped the Lord with their faces to the ground. (Nehemiah 8:_)

For A3, I5
Holding the mystery of the faith in a pure conscience. . .
(1 Timothy 3:_)

For A5, C2, G3, H7
And the time that David dwelt in the country of the Philistines was a full year and four months. (1 Samuel 27:_)

For A7, B4, F3, H6
At that time Abijah the son of Jeroboam fell sick. (1 Kings 14:_)

For B2, D6, E3
And Jesus answered and said unto them, Take heed that no man deceive you. (Matthew 24:_)

For B3, E7, H8
He that gathereth in summer is a wise son: but he that sleepeth in harvest is a son that causeth shame. (Proverbs 10:_)

For D3
And David enquired at the Lord, saying, Shall I pursue after this troop? shall I overtake them? And he answered him, Pursue: for thou shalt surely overtake them, and without fail recover all.
(1 Samuel 30:_)

For D8, F6, G9
And Joseph's ten brethren went down to buy corn in Egypt.
(Genesis 42:_)

For F9, I7
The Lord is my strength and song, and he is become my salvation: he is my God, and I will prepare him an habitation; my father's God, and I will exalt him. (Exodus 15:_)

	A	B	C	D	E	F	G	H	I
1									
2									
3									
4									
5									
6									
7									
8									
9									

Starter Numbers in Order:
6, 9, 7, 1, 4, 5, 8, 3, 2

PUZZLE 127
Medium

For A6, C1, G3, I5
And five of them were wise, and five were foolish. (Matthew 25:_)

For A8, H2, I4
Holding fast the faithful word as he hath been taught, that he may be able by sound doctrine both to exhort and to convince the gainsayers. . . (Titus 1:_)

For B1, D8, I2
So Tamar went to her brother Amnon's house; and he was laid down. And she took flour, and kneaded it, and made cakes in his sight, and did bake the cakes. (2 Samuel 13:_)

For B4, C2, D7, E6, F3, G8
And when Haman saw that Mordecai bowed not, nor did him reverence, then was Haman full of wrath. (Esther 3:_)

For B8, C5
And the LORD said, I have surely seen the affliction of my people which are in Egypt, and have heard their cry by reason of their taskmasters; for I know their sorrows. (Exodus 3:_)

For B9, D2, E5
Thou, even thou, art LORD alone; thou hast made heaven, the heaven of heavens, with all their host, the earth, and all things that are therein, the seas, and all that is therein. (Nehemiah 9:_)

For C9, E1, F8, I3
And the child Samuel ministered unto the LORD before Eli. And the word of the LORD was precious in those days; there was no open vision. (1 Samuel 3:_)

For G6, I7
And there appeared unto them cloven tongues like as of fire, and it sat upon each of them. (Acts 2:_)

For I9
I have sinned in that I have betrayed the innocent blood. And they said, What is that to us? see thou to that. (Matthew 27:_)

	A	B	C	D	E	F	G	H	I
1									
2									
3									
4									
5									
6									
7									
8									
9									

Starter Numbers in Order:
2, 9, 8, 5, 7, 6, 1, 3, 4

PUZZLE 128
Medium

	A	B	C	D	E	F	G	H	I
1								O	
2	P				E				
3	O		S	A	C			P	L
4	D			I	A		L	S	
5		I	C	L		E		A	
6		P	L	S	O			E	
7	I								
8			D		I				O
9		A		C	S		I		E

Hint: Column E

And there followed him great multitudes of people from Galilee, and from _____, and from Jerusalem, and from Judaea, and from beyond Jordan. (Matthew 4:25)

	A	B	C	D	E	F	G	H	I
1			Y					H	
2	B	R		A	T		Y		
3					Y		E	R	
4	U		O				H		
5						E		B	O
6	A			R					
7	R	A						T	
8				T				U	
9	E		T	U	H				B

Hint: Row 2

Thus saith the Lord GOD unto these bones; Behold, I will cause
_____ to enter into ___, and ye shall live. (Ezekiel 37:5)

Fun BIBLE **SUDOKU 2**

	A	B	C	D	E	F	G	H	I
1				W		B			U
2	B				E				
3	W				I	T		E	D
4		U		B				D	
5							K		
6	I		K			C			E
7				W	K				C
8		W						B	
9		E		I	B	D			

Hint: Column F

He will keep the feet of his saints, and/____ the _____ shall be silent in darkness. (1 Samuel 2:9)

	A	B	C	D	E	F	G	H	I
1			U	I			L		
2			E						U
3	D	I				G			F
4		A		G					D
5		E						L	
6				A					
7	I	F					U		L
8	G			R	D				E
9		L	R			U	G		

Hint: Row 8

And a flaming sword which turned every way, to keep/_____ the way of the tree of _____. (Genesis 3:24)

PUZZLE 132
Difficult

For A3, B5, D8
Now the name of the man was Nabal; and the name of his wife Abigail: and she was a woman of good understanding, and of a beautiful countenance. (1 Samuel 25:_)

For A9, D3, F5, G4, I7
Repent ye: for the kingdom of heaven is at hand. (Matthew 3:_)

For B2, E5
From the first day of the seventh month began they to offer burnt offerings unto the LORD. But the foundation of the temple of the LORD was not yet laid. (Ezra 3:_)

For B6, D1, E4, I9
And the men which journeyed with him stood speechless, hearing a voice, but seeing no man. (Acts 9:_)

For B7, D4, I2
Blessed is the man that walketh not in the counsel of the ungodly, nor standeth in the way of sinners, nor sitteth in the seat of the scornful. (Psalm 1:_)

For B9, C3, G1
But Zadok the priest, and Benaiah the son of Jehoiada, and Nathan the prophet, and Shimei, and Rei, and the mighty men which belonged to David, were not with Adonijah. (1 Kings 1:_)

For C5, D7
Then the king said, Cause Haman to make haste, that he may do as Esther hath said. So the king and Haman came to the banquet that Esther had prepared. (Esther 5:_)

For D2, F7, I5
But Jesus, said unto them, A prophet is not without honour, but in his own country, and among his own kin, and in his own house. (Mark 6:_)

For F9
But, beloved, we are persuaded better things of you, and things that accompany salvation, though we thus speak. (Hebrews 6:_)

	A	B	C	D	E	F	G	H	I
1									
2									
3									
4									
5									
6									
7									
8									
9									

Starter Numbers in Order:
3, 2, 6, 7, 1, 8, 5, 4, 9

PUZZLE 133
Difficult

For A1, C8, G9
And spared not the old world, but saved Noah the eighth person, a
preacher of righteousness, bringing in the flood upon the world of
the ungodly. . . (2 Peter 2:_)

For A9, B5, F3, H7
But in all this time was not I at Jerusalem: for in the two and
thirtieth year of Artaxerxes king of Babylon came I unto the king,
and after certain days obtained I leave of the king. (Nehemiah 13:_)

For B2, F9, G3, H6
And there they preached the gospel. (Acts 14:_)

For B3, C6, G1, I9
And Nathan said to the king, Go, do all that is in thine heart; for
the LORD is with thee. (2 Samuel 7:_)

For B6, E8, G5
And after six days Jesus taketh with him Peter, and James, and
John, and leadeth them up into an high mountain apart by
themselves: and he was transfigured before them. (Mark 9:_)

For B7, I1
And the ark of the LORD was in the country of the Philistines
seven months. (1 Samuel 6:_)

For B8, D9, I5
And, behold, thou has with thee Shimei the son of Gera, a
Benjamite of Bahurim, which cursed me with a grievous curse in
the day when I went to Mahanaim. (1 Kings 2:_)

For E1
Jesus saith unto her, Woman, what have I to do with thee? mine
hour is not yet come. (John 2:_)

For E2, I3
Grudge not one against another, brethren, lest ye be condemned:
behold, the judge standeth before the door. (James 5:_)

	A	B	C	D	E	F	G	H	I
1									
2									
3									
4									
5									
6									
7									
8									
9									

Starter Numbers in Order:
5, 6, 7, 3, 2, 1, 8, 4, 9

PUZZLE 134
Difficult

For A2, F8, I5
And the anger of the LORD was kindled against Uzzah; and God smote him there for his error; and there he died by the ark of God. (2 Samuel 6:_)

For B1, F4
Surely goodness and mercy shall follow me all the days of my life: and I will dwell in the house of the LORD for ever. (Psalm 23:_)

For B5, H7, I6
For the LORD will have mercy on Jacob, and will yet choose Israel, and set them in their own land. (Isaiah 14:_)

For B6, F1, H9
And the LORD said unto him, I have heard thy prayer and thy supplication, that thou hast made before me: I have hallowed this house, which thou hast built. (1 Kings 9:_)

For B9, E6, H1
When Jesus heard that, he said, This sickness is not unto death, but for the glory of God, that the Son of God might be glorified thereby. (John 11:_)

For C3, D2, E4, G8
And being made perfect, he became the author of eternal salvation unto all them that obey him. (Hebrews 5:_)

For C6, E7
And Pilate asked him, Are thou the King of the Jews? And he answering said unto them, Thou sayest it. (Mark 15:_)

For D3, F6
And there was war again: and David went out, and fought with the Philistines, and slew them with a great slaughter; and they fled from him. (1 Samuel 19:_)

For F7, H6
He that overcometh, the same shall be clothed in white raiment; and I will not blot out his name out of the book of life, but I will confess his name before my Father, and before his angels. (Revelation 3:_)

	A	B	C	D	E	F	G	H	I
1									
2									
3									
4									
5									
6									
7									
8									
9									

Starter Numbers in Order:
7, 6, 1, 3, 4, 9, 2, 8, 5

PUZZLE 135
Difficult

	A	B	C	D	E	F	G	H	I
1	C		S				U		
2		H	E					O	
3				T	H	O			E
4			R			H			
5	O	T		U				A	
6			H					R	
7		C			T				U
8	H				S				O
9		E	T				S	C	

Hint: Column C

Behold, there came men in hither to night of the children of Israel to _____ ___ the country. (Joshua 2:2)

	A	B	C	D	E	F	G	H	I
1		E			D	N			L
2			R			I			
3	A	D	H		T				
4	T			I		L			D
5	D	L							R
6				T					
7	N			D		H	T	I	A
8				A				H	
9					L				E

Hint: Row 4

Though _____ _____ was filled with sin against the Holy One of Israel. . . (Jeremiah 51:5)

PUZZLE 137
Difficult

For A2, I6
And Solomon had twelve officers over all Israel, which provided victuals for the king and his household: each man his month in a year made provision. (1 Kings 4:_)

For B2, D1
Who is he that overcometh the world, but he that believeth that Jesus is the Son of God? (1 John 5:_)

For B3, D2, G7
And they remembered his words. (Luke 24:_)

For B5, D6, F1, H2
So they ran both together: and the other disciple did outrun Peter, and came first to the sepulchre. (John 20:_)

For B7, E6
And he had seven hundred wives, princesses, and three hundred concubines: and his wives turned away his heart. (1 Kings 11:_)

For B8, D5, G3
I AM the man that hath seen affliction by the rod of his wrath. (Lamentations 3:_)

For C4, D7
And he said unto me, It is done. I am Alpha and Omega, the beginning and the end. I will give unto him that is athirst of the fountain of the water of life freely. (Revelation 21:_)

For E9, H3
But if ye have respect to persons, ye commit sin, and are convinced of the law as transgressors. (James 2:_)

For G2, I4
Thou art snared with the words of thy mouth, thou art taken with the words of thy mouth. (Proverbs 6:_)

	A	B	C	D	E	F	G	H	I
1									
2									
3									
4									
5									
6									
7									
8									
9									

Starter Numbers in Order:
7, 5, 8, 4, 3, 1, 6, 9, 2

PUZZLE 138
Difficult

For A2, B5, F3, H1
Go to the ant, thou sluggard; consider her ways, and be wise.
(Proverbs 6:_)

For A3, C6
There cometh a woman of Samaria to draw water: Jesus saith unto
her, Give me to drink. (John 4:_)

For A8, C5, G2
And there were four leprous men at the entering in of the gate: and
they said one to another, Why sit we here until we die? (2 Kings 7:_)

For A9, D6, I5
And they were all filled with the Holy Ghost, and began to speak
with other tongues, as the Spirit gave them utterance. (Acts 2:_)

For B2, D8, H7
But he forsook the counsel of the old men, which they had given
him, and consulted with the young men that were grown up with
him, and which stood before him. (1 Kings 12:_)

For C2, D3, F7, I1
For this cause we also, since the day we heard it, do not cease
to pray for you, and to desire that ye might be filled with the
knowledge of his will in all wisdom and spiritual understanding.
(Colossians 1:_)

For D9, F1
Now there was long war between the house of Saul and the house
of David. (2 Samuel 3:_)

For E8
For there is nothing covered, that shall not be revealed; neither
hid, that shall not be known. (Luke 12:_)

For H4, I9
And if any man will hurt them, fire proceedeth out of their mouth,
and devoureth their enemies: and if any man will hurt them, he
must in this manner be killed. (Revelation 11:_)

	A	B	C	D	E	F	G	H	I
1									
2									
3									
4									
5									
6									
7									
8									
9									

Starter Numbers in Order:
6, 7, 3, 4, 8, 9, 1, 2, 5

PUZZLE 139
Difficult

For A4, B3
But neither Titus, who was with me, being a Greek, was compelled to be circumcised. (Galatians 2:_)

For A9, C3, E4, H7
And there went out a champion out of the camp of the Philistines, named Goliath, of Gath. (1 Samuel 17:_)

For B2, D1, H4
And Nathan said to David, Thou art the man. Thus saith the LORD God of Israel, I anointed thee king over Israel, and I delivered thee out of the hand of Saul. (2 Samuel 12:_)

For B4, G6, H8, I2
Now there is at Jerusalem by the sheep market a pool, which is called in the Hebrew tongue Bethesda, having five porches. (John 5:_)

For C1, D5, I8
And he that sat upon the throne said, Behold, I make all things new. And he said unto me, Write: for these words are true and faithful. (Revelation 21:_)

For C6, E9, G8
Train up a child in the way he should go: and when he is old, he will not depart from it. (Proverbs 22:_)

For C8, E2
Lie not one to another, seeing that ye have put off the old man with his deeds. (Colossians 3:_)

For D7, E1
The words of Amos, who was among the herdmen of Tekoa, which he saw concerning Israel. . .two years before the earthquake. . . (Amos 1:_)

For F8, G5, I1
Now the rest of the acts of Jehoahaz, and all that he did, and his might, are they not written in the book of the chronicles of the kings of Israel? (2 Kings 13:_)

	A	B	C	D	E	F	G	H	I
1									
2									
3									
4									
5									
6									
7									
8									
9									

Starter Numbers in Order:
3, 4, 7, 2, 5, 6, 9, 1, 8

PUZZLE 140
Difficult

	A	B	C	D	E	F	G	H	I
1	O			L			A		F
2		F						D	
3	D	A	L	F			N		
4		E	R						W
5									
6		W		E		D	O	N	
7	W		O			N	L		A
8		R	F						N
9					W	A	R		

Hint: Column I

He cometh forth like a _____, ___ is cut down: he fleeth also as a shadow, and continueth not. (Job 14:2)

	A	B	C	D	E	F	G	H	I
1	W				U			R	Y
2			G						
3	H			G			W		
4	S	W		U			R		A
5				S	N	H			
6				W		R			
7			W						G
8		U					N	S	
9			A			U			

Hint: Row 1

After fasting forty days and forty nights, he ___ _____.
(Matthew 4:2 NIV)

PUZZLE 142
Difficult

For A1, B7, F9
For what thanks can we render to God again for you, for all the joy wherewith we joy for your sakes before our God? (1 Thessalonians 3:_)

For A6, E2, G5, H7
We are troubled on every side, yet not distressed; we are perplexed, but not in despair. (2 Corinthians 4:_)

For A8, E5, I3
Howbeit I believed not the words, until I came, and mine eyes had seen it: and, behold, the half was not told me: thy wisdom and prosperity exceedeth the fame which I heard. (1 Kings 10:_)

For A9, D6
And he that sat was to look upon like a jasper and a sardine stone: and there was a rainbow round about the throne, in sight like unto an emerald. (Revelation 4:_)

For B1, D9, G4, H3
A wise man will hear, and will increase learning; and a man of understanding shall attain unto wise counsels. (Proverbs 1:_)

For B3, D1, H8
Therefore they that were scattered abroad went every where preaching the word. (Acts 8:_)

For B4, D2
And Ahab told Jezebel all that Elijah had done, and withal how he had slain all the prophets with the sword. (1 Kings 19:_)

For D5
So Jacob came to Luz, which is in the land of Canaan, that is, Bethel, he and all the people that were with him. (Genesis 35:_)

For F7, G9, H2
And a certain man lame from his mother's womb was carried, whom they laid daily at the gate of the temple which is called Beautiful, to ask alms of them that entered into the temple. (Acts 3:_)

	A	B	C	D	E	F	G	H	I
1									
2									
3									
4									
5									
6									
7									
8									
9									

Starter Numbers in Order:
9, 8, 7, 3, 5, 4, 1, 6, 2

PUZZLE 143
Difficult

For A1, D5, H2
And devout men carried Stephen to his burial, and made great lamentation over him. (Acts 8:_)

For A2, F9, G8
The same day went Jesus out of the house, and sat by the sea side. (Matthew 13:_)

For A6, F1, H7
Blessings are upon the head of the just: but violence covereth the mouth of the wicked. (Proverbs 10:_)

For A9, I7
Thou shalt not take the name of the LORD thy God in vain; for the LORD will not hold him guiltless that taketh his name in vain. (Exodus 20:_)

For B7, E2, G6
For God hath not appointed us to wrath, but to obtain salvation by our Lord Jesus Christ. (1 Thessalonians 5:_)

For B8, C3, H4
Who are kept by the power of God through faith unto salvation ready to be revealed in the last time. . . (1 Peter 1:_)

For C1
For by grace are ye saved through faith; and that not of yourselves: it is the gift of God. (Ephesians 2:_)

For D2, E6, G3
And all went to be taxed, every one into his own city. (Luke 2:_)

For E4, H9
And Jonathan stripped himself of the robe that was upon him, and gave it to David, and his garments, even to his sword, and to his bow, and to his girdle. (1 Samuel 18:_)

	A	B	C	D	E	F	G	H	I
1									
2									
3									
4									
5									
6									
7									
8									
9									

Starter Numbers in Order:
2, 1, 6, 7, 9, 5, 8, 3, 4

PUZZLE 144
Difficult

For A1, B6, I8
For better it is that it be said unto thee, Come up hither; than that thou shouldest be put lower in the presence of the prince whom thine eyes have seen. (Proverbs 25:_)

For A3, E7, I9
Ye have lived in pleasure on the earth, and been wanton; ye have nourished your hearts, as in a day of slaughter. (James 5:_)

For A9, B1, E2
And finding a ship sailing over unto Phenicia, we went aboard, and set forth. (Acts 21:_)

For B4, F1, H7
And Joseph was the governor over the land, and he it was that sold to all the people of the land. (Genesis 42:_)

For B7, G9, H3, I5
And it came to pass in those days, that there went out a decree from Caesar Augustus that all the world should be taxed. (Luke 2:_)

For C2, F5, H1, I6
And he fell to the earth, and heard a voice saying unto him, Saul, Saul, why persecutest thou me? (Acts 9:_)

For C7, I1
And if I go and prepare a place for you, I will come again, and receive you unto myself; that where I am, there ye may be also. (John 14:_)

For C8, I3
And this I pray, that your love may abound yet more and more in knowledge and in all judgment. (Philippians 1:_)

For E5, F9
Knowing that whatsoever good thing any man doeth, the same shall he receive of the Lord, whether he be bond or free. (Ephesians 6:_)

	A	B	C	D	E	F	G	H	I
1									
2									
3									
4									
5									
6									
7									
8									
9									

Starter Numbers in Order:
7, 5, 2, 6, 1, 4, 3, 9, 8

PUZZLE 145
Difficult

	A	B	C	D	E	F	G	H	I
1			H	M	E			O	U
2	A						M	F	
3		T	M			F			
4	H				M	C	U	E	
5				H					
6	M			F					
7		E	O				F		
8	U			C		O		H	T
9		H					A		

Hint: Column D

As the word went out of the king's _____, they covered Haman's
_____. (Esther 7:8)

	A	B	C	D	E	F	G	H	I
1	U		B		D	S	L		R
2									S
3		C						O	
4		B							
5		D		W	L	O			C
6							R		
7	C	L		B	S			R	
8		R	O						
9		S		R			C		B

Hint: Row 7

A man that beareth false witness against his neighbour is a
maul/_____, and a _____, and a sharp arrow. (Proverbs 25:18)

PUZZLE 147
Difficult

For A3, E6, F7, G1
Even so the tongue is a little member, and boasteth great things.
Behold, how great a matter a little fire kindleth! (James 3:_)

For B4, C9, D1
And when they heard that he spake in the Hebrew tongue to
them, they kept the more silence. (Acts 22:_)

For B7, C3, E9
And my speech and my preaching was not with enticing words
of man's wisdom. (1 Corinthians 2:_)

For B9, G3, H7
And it came to pass, that, as he was praying in a certain place,
when he ceased, one of his disciples said unto him, Lord, teach
us to pray, as John also taught his disciples. (Luke 11:_)

For C6, D3, E5
And being found in fashion as a man, he humbled himself,
and became obedient unto death, even the death of the cross.
(Philippians 2:_)

For E4, F1
And all flesh shall see the salvation of God. (Luke 3:_)

For E7, I5
Not of works, lest any man should boast. . . (Ephesians 2:_)

For G6, H1
And the battle went sore against Saul, and the archers hit him;
and he was sore wounded of the archers. (1 Samuel 31:_)

For H9
The just man walketh in his integrity: his children are blessed after
him. (Proverbs 20:_)

	A	B	C	D	E	F	G	H	I
1									
2									
3									
4									
5									
6									
7									
8									
9									

Starter Numbers in Order:
5, 2, 4, 1, 8, 6, 9, 3, 7

Fun BIBLE **SUDOKU 2**

PUZZLE 148
Difficult

For A2, F6, G7
These words spake Jesus, and lifted up his eyes to heaven, and said, Father, the hour is come; glorify thy Son, that thy Son also may glorify thee. (John 17:_)

For A7, B6, D3, E9
The wise in heart will receive commandments: but a prating fool shall fall. (Proverbs 10:_)

For B2, D5, I1
And there shall be no night there; and they need no candle, neither light of the sun; for the Lord God giveth them light: and they shall reign for ever and ever. (Revelation 22:_)

For B7, C1, I9
And some fell upon a rock; and as soon as it was sprung up, it withered away, because it lacked moisture. (Luke 8:_)

For D6, E2, H3, I4
And Naboth said to Ahab, The LORD forbid it me, that I should give the inheritance of my fathers unto thee. (1 Kings 21:_)

For D8, F1, H4
Rejoice in the Lord always: and again I say, Rejoice. (Philippians 4:_)

For E4
For the fruit of the Spirit is in all goodness and righteousness and truth. (Ephesians 5:_)

For E6, F8, I3
And they found the stone rolled away from the sepulchre. (Luke 24:_)

For G9
And the king said unto the man of God, Come home with me, and refresh thyself, and I will give thee a reward. (1 Kings 13:_)

	A	B	C	D	E	F	G	H	I
1									
2									
3									
4									
5									
6									
7									
8									
9									

Starter Numbers in Order:
1, 8, 5, 6, 3, 4, 9, 2, 7

PUZZLE 149
Difficult

For A4, B7, E9
And she said unto her mistress, Would God my lord were with the
prophet that is in Samaria! for he would recover him of his leprosy.
(2 Kings 5:_)

For A6, B9, E5, I2
Happy are thy men, happy are these thy servants, which stand
continually before thee, and that hear thy wisdom. (1 Kings 10:_)

For A9, B6, D5, G3
And it came to pass after a while, that the brook dried up, because
there had been no rain in the land. (1 Kings 17:_)

For C5, H6, I1
And Jesus said, Let her alone; why trouble ye her? she hath
wrought a good work on me. (Mark 14:_)

For C7, I5
And he wept aloud: and the Egyptians and the house of Pharaoh
heard. (Genesis 45:_)

For C8, E6, G1
Having made known unto us the mystery of his will, according
to his good pleasure which he hath purposed in himself. . .
(Ephesians 1:_)

For D3, G5
And these things write we unto you, that your joy may be full.
(1 John 1:_)

For D7, F5
Now I will come unto you, when I shall pass through Macedonia:
for I do pass through Macedonia. (1 Corinthians 16:_)

For F1, H3, I6
Now when Solomon had made an end of praying, the fire came down
from heaven, and consumed the burnt offering and the sacrifices;
and the glory of the LORD filled the house. (2 Chronicles 7:_)

	A	B	C	D	E	F	G	H	I
1									
2									
3									
4									
5									
6									
7									
8									
9									

Starter Numbers in Order:
3, 8, 7, 6, 2, 9, 4, 5, 1

PUZZLE 150
Difficult

	A	B	C	D	E	F	G	H	I
1				Y					O
2	T	Y	R	E				I	
3		P		H		I			
4	E								Y
5					E				
6		R	H	C			O		P
7							Y		R
8	R					Y			
9			P	O			C	T	I

Hint: Column B

Thou _____, first cast out the beam out of thine own eye.
(Matthew 7:5)

	A	B	C	D	E	F	G	H	I
1				O		D		I	G
2								O	R
3				I	S		A		
4	E					G	I	D	
5	I				R	E			
6					A				
7		R	L						
8			S	A		L			
9	A	G		R		O			

Hint: Row 3

Indeed I have sinned against the LORD ___ of _____.
(Joshua 7:20)

PUZZLE 152
Difficult

For A1, C7
Examine yourselves, whether ye be in the faith; prove your own selves. Know ye not your own selves, how that Jesus Christ is in you, except ye be reprobates? (2 Corinthians 13:_)

For A2, B5, D4, E3
And the angel of the LORD came again the second time, and touched him, and said, Arise and eat; because the journey is too great for thee. (1 Kings 19:_)

For A6, D5, F8, I2
The Spirit of God came upon Azariah the son of Oded. (2 Chronicles 15:_)

For A7, D3, E8, F6, G9
And he said unto me, My grace is sufficient for thee: for my strength is made perfect in weakness. (2 Corinthians 12:_)

For A9, C6, E2, H5
A fool hath no delight in understanding, but that his heart may discover itself. (Proverbs 18:_)

For C2, D6, E9, G5
And when he cometh home, he calleth together his friends and neighbours, saying unto them, Rejoice with me; for I have found my sheep which was lost. (Luke 15:_)

For D1, H3, I7
And the king of Israel said unto Jehoshaphat, There is yet one man, Micaiah the son of Imlah, by whom we may enquire of the LORD: but I hate him. (1 Kings 22:_)

For E4, G2, H7
For the weapons of our warfare are not carnal, but mighty through God to the pulling down of strong holds. (2 Corinthians 10:_)

For E7, F5, G6
For if a man think himself to be something, when he is nothing, he deceiveth himself. (Galatians 6:_)

	A	B	C	D	E	F	G	H	I
1									
2									
3									
4									
5									
6									
7									
8									
9									

Starter Numbers in Order:
5, 7, 1, 9, 2, 6, 8, 4, 3

PUZZLE 153
Difficult

For A4, F3
Where no oxen are, the crib is clean: but much increase is by the strength of the ox. (Proverbs 14:_)

For A5, C7
And it came to pass, when Hiram heard the words of Solomon, that he rejoiced greatly, and said, Blessed be the Lord this day, which hath given unto David a wise son over this great people. (1 Kings 5:_)

For A7, C1, E5
And Moses said, I will now turn aside, and see this great sight, why the bush is not burnt. (Exodus 3:_)

For B2, D9, G5, I7
And Sarah said, God hath made me to laugh, so that all that hear will laugh with me. (Genesis 21:_)

For B6, D7, F5, G3
Hear me when I call, O God of my righteousness: thou hast enlarged me when I was in distress; have mercy upon me, and hear my prayer. (Psalm 4:_)

For C3, H5, I8
A little leaven leaveneth the whole lump. (Galatians 5:_)

For E6, F1, H4
And they answered him, He was an hairy man, and girt with a girdle of leather about his loins. And he said, It is Elijah the Tishbite. (2 Kings 1:_)

For F6, I1
To him be glory for ever and ever. Amen. (Galatians 1:_)

For G9
For yourselves know perfectly that the day of the Lord so cometh as a thief in the night. (1 Thessalonians 5:_)

	A	B	C	D	E	F	G	H	I
1									
2									
3									
4									
5									
6									
7									
8									
9									

Starter Numbers in Order:
4, 7, 3, 6, 1, 9, 8, 5, 2

PUZZLE 154
Difficult

For A1, E5, F8
Then she came and told the man of God. And he said, Go, sell the oil, and pay thy debt, and live thou and thy children of the rest. (2 Kings 4:_)

For A2, C6, G5
Then was Jesus led up of the Spirit into the wilderness to be tempted of the devil. (Matthew 4:_)

For A4, I9
And I saw a strong angel proclaiming with a loud voice, Who is worthy to open the book, and to loose the seals thereof? (Revelation 5:_)

For A9, C3, H8
And Abraham circumcised his son Isaac being eight days old, as God had commanded him. (Genesis 21:_)

For C1, E2, H6
And he said, Which way shall we go up? And he answered, The way through the wilderness of Edom. (2 Kings 3:_)

For D3, F6, I2
For how can I endure to see the evil that shall come unto my people? or how can I endure to see the destruction of my kindred? (Esther 8:_)

For D8, I5
And ye have forgotten the exhortation which speaketh unto you as unto children, My son, despise not thou the chastening of the Lord, nor faint when thou art rebuked of him. (Hebrews 12:_)

For F2, H1, I8
And David went thence to Mizpeh of Moab: and he said unto the king of Moab, Let my father and my mother, I pray thee, come forth, and be with you, till I know what God will do for me. (1 Samuel 22:_)

For F3, G7
That I may not seem as if I would terrify you by letters. . . (2 Corinthians 10:_)

	A	B	C	D	E	F	G	H	I
1									
2									
3									
4									
5									
6									
7									
8									
9									

Starter Numbers in Order:
7, 1, 2, 4, 8, 6, 5, 3, 9

PUZZLE 155
Difficult

For A1, F9, H8, I3
And there went out another horse that was red. (Revelation 6:_)

For A3, C9, H7
Cast thy bread upon the waters: for thou shalt find it after many days. (Ecclesiastes 11:_)

For A5, D3, H2, I7
Jesus answered, Neither hath this man sinned, nor his parents: but that the works of God should be made manifest in him. (John 9:_)

For B6, D2, F8
For true and righteous are his judgments: for he hath judged the great whore, which did corrupt the earth with her fornication, and hath avenged the blood of his servants at her hand. (Revelation 19:_)

For B7, C2, D8, I4
And when these lepers came to the uttermost part of the camp, they went into one tent, and did eat and drink, and carried thence silver, and gold, and raiment, and went and hid it. (2 Kings 7:_)

For B8, C5, E3
Persecuted, but not forsaken; cast down, but not destroyed. . .
(2 Corinthians 4:_)

For B9, I2
For her sins have reached unto heaven, and God hath remembered her iniquities. (Revelation 18:_)

For G5
And Jehoshaphat said, Is there not here a prophet of the LORD besides, that we might enquire of him? (1 Kings 22:_)

For H4, I1
O my God, I am ashamed and blush to lift up my face to thee, my God: for our iniquities are increased over our head, and our trespass is grown up unto the heavens. (Ezra 9:_)

	A	B	C	D	E	F	G	H	I
1									
2									
3									
4									
5									
6									
7									
8									
9									

Starter Numbers in Order:
4, 1, 3, 2, 8, 9, 5, 7, 6

PUZZLE 156
Difficult

For A1, D3, E7, I2
But we had the sentence of death in ourselves, that we should not trust in ourselves, but in God which raiseth the dead. (2 Corinthians 1:_)

For A5, C8, E1
Thou therefore endure hardness, as a good soldier of Jesus Christ. (2 Timothy 2:_)

For A6, I9
All this was done, that it might be fulfilled which was spoken by the prophet. (Matthew 21:_)

For A9, D4, G7, I1
A wise man is strong; yea, a man of knowledge increaseth strength. (Proverbs 24:_)

For B1, D2, G4
And I was very angry when I heard their cry and these words. (Nehemiah 5:_)

For B4, D9, I5
Wisdom is too high for a fool: he openeth not his mouth in the gate. (Proverbs 24:_)

For B8, F9
Looking unto Jesus the author and finisher of our faith; who for the joy that was set before him endured the cross, despising the shame, and is set down at the right hand of the throne of God. . . (Hebrews 12:_)

For C9, E6, G3
Judge not, that ye be not judged. (Matthew 7:_)

For E9, G6, H1
And Ahaz took the silver and gold that was found in the house of the LORD, and in the treasures of the king's house, and sent it for a present to the king of Assyria. (2 Kings 16:_)

	A	B	C	D	E	F	G	H	I
1									
2									
3									
4									
5									
6									
7									
8									
9									

Starter Numbers in Order:
9, 3, 4, 5, 6, 7, 2, 1, 8

PUZZLE 157
Difficult

For A1, C7
For I am the least of the apostles, that am not meet to be
called an apostle, because I persecuted the church of God.
(1 Corinthians 15:_)

For A3, E8, I1
Now in Shushan the palace there was a certain Jew, whose name
was Mordecai. (Esther 2:_)

For A9, E6
It is an honour for a man to cease from strife: but every fool will
be meddling. (Proverbs 20:_)

For B7, C4, H6
That ye be not soon shaken in mind, or be troubled, neither by
spirit, nor by word, nor by letter as from us, as that the day of
Christ is at hand. . . (2 Thessalonians 2:_)

For B8, E2
Now faith is the substance of things hoped for, the evidence of
things not seen. (Hebrews 11:_)

For C6, G8, I2
By humility and the fear of the LORD are riches, and honour, and
life. (Proverbs 22:_)

For D6, E9, H1
He smote the Philistines, even unto Gaza, and the borders thereof,
from the tower of the watchmen to the fenced city. (2 Kings 18:_)

For E5, I3
In all thy ways acknowledge him, and he shall direct thy paths.
(Proverbs 3:_)

For F1, G9, I6
Beareth all things, believeth all things, hopeth all things, endureth
all things. . . (1 Corinthians 13:_)

	A	B	C	D	E	F	G	H	I
1									
2									
3									
4									
5									
6									
7									
8									
9									

Starter Numbers in Order:
9, 5, 3, 2, 1, 4, 8, 6, 7

PUZZLE 158
Difficult

For A7, C3, F9, I2
But take heed lest by any means this liberty of yours become a stumblingblock to them that are weak. (1 Corinthians 8:_)

For A8, G5
All things were made by him; and without him was not any thing made that was made. (John 1:_)

For B2, C7, E5
And the priests consented to receive no more money of the people, neither to repair the breaches of the house. (2 Kings 12:_)

For B6, E1, H8, I5
And there the centurion found a ship of Alexandria sailing into Italy; and he put us therein. (Acts 27:_)

For C9, E4, H2
A good man obtaineth favour of the LORD: but a man of wicked devices will he condemn. (Proverbs 12:_)

For D4, E3, G2
Then Naomi her mother in law said unto her, My daughter, shall I not seek rest for thee, that it may be well with thee? (Ruth 3:_)

For E2, F7
Walk in wisdom toward them that are without, redeeming the time. (Colossians 4:_)

For F2, H4
But made himself of no reputation, and took upon him the form of a servant, and was made in the likeness of men. . . (Philippians 2:_)

For F5, H7
And that he was buried, and that he rose again the third day according to the scriptures. . . (1 Corinthians 15:_)

	A	B	C	D	E	F	G	H	I
1									
2									
3									
4									
5									
6									
7									
8									
9									

Starter Numbers in Order:
9, 3, 8, 6, 2, 1, 5, 7, 4

PUZZLE 159
Difficult

For A3, C7, F1, G2
I will praise thee, O Lord, with my whole heart; I will shew forth all thy marvellous works. (Psalm 9:_)

For A6, C1, G8
And there came a messenger, and told him, saying, They have brought the heads of the king's sons. And he said, Lay ye them in two heaps at the entering in of the gate until the morning. (2 Kings 10:_)

For A7, G9, H6
And they entered in, and found not the body of the Lord Jesus. (Luke 24:_)

For B1, E7, I4
He riseth from supper, and laid aside his garments; and took a towel, and girded himself. (John 13:_)

For B2, F7, I8
In whom we have redemption through his blood, the forgiveness of sins, according to the riches of his grace. . . (Ephesians 1:_)

For B6, E4
For the Lord giveth wisdom: out of his mouth cometh knowledge and understanding. (Proverbs 2:_)

For B8, G1
One Lord, one faith, one baptism. . . (Ephesians 4:_)

For B9, H2
For in this we groan, earnestly desiring to be clothed upon with our house which is from heaven. (2 Corinthians 5:_)

For D3, E6, G7, I1
For we are labourers together with God: ye are God's husbandry, ye are God's building. (1 Corinthians 3:_)

	A	B	C	D	E	F	G	H	I
1									
2									
3									
4									
5									
6									
7									
8									
9									

Starter Numbers in Order:
1, 8, 3, 4, 7, 6, 5, 2, 9

PUZZLE 160
Difficult

	A	B	C	D	E	F	G	H	I
1		S	D		O	M	W		
2			Y					R	D
3						N			
4	N					Y			
5					M	W			Y
6			R	S			A		
7			A		N	R	Y		
8	M					D			
9	O							D	A

Hint: Column F

For they think that they shall be heard for their much/_____ speaking/_____. (Matthew 6:7)

ANSWERS

R	L	D	S	E	F	I	H	O
I	O	F	D	R	H	S	E	L
H	E	S	O	I	L	R	D	F
F	D	E	I	O	R	L	S	H
L	R	O	F	H	S	E	I	D
S	H	I	E	L	D	F	O	R
O	S	R	H	F	E	D	L	I
D	F	H	L	S	I	O	R	E
E	I	L	R	D	O	H	F	S

PUZZLE 1

1	8	5	9	3	2	6	4	7
9	2	4	8	6	7	3	1	5
7	3	6	4	5	1	2	8	9
8	9	2	3	7	4	1	5	6
5	6	3	1	8	9	7	2	4
4	7	1	5	2	6	8	9	3
2	5	8	6	9	3	4	7	1
6	4	9	7	1	8	5	3	2
3	1	7	2	4	5	9	6	8

PUZZLE 2

1	9	3	7	5	8	6	2	4
2	8	7	4	3	6	9	1	5
4	6	5	1	2	9	7	3	8
9	1	2	5	7	3	4	8	6
5	7	8	2	6	4	3	9	1
3	4	6	9	8	1	2	5	7
6	5	1	3	4	2	8	7	9
8	2	9	6	1	7	5	4	3
7	3	4	8	9	5	1	6	2

PUZZLE 3

2	1	5	6	8	3	7	9	4
4	7	8	1	2	9	6	5	3
3	6	9	7	4	5	8	2	1
8	4	7	9	1	2	3	6	5
5	3	2	8	7	6	4	1	9
6	9	1	5	3	4	2	8	7
9	8	3	2	5	7	1	4	6
1	5	4	3	6	8	9	7	2
7	2	6	4	9	1	5	3	8

PUZZLE 4

H	I	V	F	W	O	T	A	R
O	T	W	A	R	H	I	F	V
F	R	A	V	I	T	W	H	O
R	W	T	O	H	I	A	V	F
V	O	F	R	T	A	H	W	I
I	A	H	W	F	V	O	R	T
T	H	R	I	V	W	F	O	A
W	V	O	T	A	F	R	I	H
A	F	I	H	O	R	V	T	W

PUZZLE 5

S	O	M	E	T	H	I	N	G
I	E	T	G	N	S	M	O	H
H	N	G	O	M	I	S	T	E
E	S	N	I	O	M	G	H	T
M	G	H	T	S	N	E	I	O
O	T	I	H	E	G	N	M	S
N	M	O	S	H	E	T	G	I
T	I	S	M	G	O	H	E	N
G	H	E	N	I	T	O	S	M

PUZZLE 6

4	8	5	6	9	3	2	1	7
7	1	6	8	5	2	4	3	9
3	9	2	4	7	1	6	8	5
1	5	7	2	8	4	3	9	6
2	6	4	3	1	9	5	7	8
8	3	9	7	6	5	1	4	2
6	4	1	9	2	8	7	5	3
5	2	8	1	3	7	9	6	4
9	7	3	5	4	6	8	2	1

PUZZLE 7

9	5	3	6	2	7	1	8	4
6	7	4	1	8	9	5	3	2
8	2	1	3	5	4	7	6	9
4	3	2	8	6	5	9	7	1
5	8	7	9	4	1	3	2	6
1	9	6	7	3	2	8	4	5
3	1	8	2	9	6	4	5	7
2	4	9	5	7	3	6	1	8
7	6	5	4	1	8	2	9	3

PUZZLE 8

Fᴜɴ BIBLE SUDOKU 2

PUZZLE 9

8	3	5	9	1	7	4	2	6
9	7	6	8	2	4	1	3	5
1	4	2	6	5	3	9	8	7
5	1	7	2	4	9	3	6	8
3	2	9	5	6	8	7	1	4
4	6	8	3	7	1	5	9	2
2	9	4	1	8	5	6	7	3
7	8	1	4	3	6	2	5	9
6	5	3	7	9	2	8	4	1

PUZZLE 10

L	H	F	M	I	S	E	T	O
E	I	T	O	H	L	F	M	S
O	M	S	E	F	T	I	H	L
I	S	O	H	L	M	T	E	F
F	E	M	S	T	O	L	I	H
T	L	H	I	E	F	S	O	M
H	F	L	T	O	E	M	S	I
M	T	I	F	S	H	O	L	E
S	O	E	L	M	I	H	F	T

PUZZLE 11

O	C	U	E	N	R	L	S	I
E	S	N	I	L	C	U	O	R
L	R	I	U	S	O	E	C	N
C	O	R	N	E	L	I	U	S
S	I	L	O	C	U	N	R	E
N	U	E	R	I	S	O	L	C
R	N	C	L	O	I	S	E	U
U	E	O	S	R	N	C	I	L
I	L	S	C	U	E	R	N	O

PUZZLE 12

3	2	9	5	8	7	1	6	4
8	6	4	9	3	1	7	2	5
1	5	7	6	2	4	3	9	8
9	3	6	7	4	8	2	5	1
4	7	1	3	5	2	6	8	9
5	8	2	1	6	9	4	7	3
2	1	3	8	9	6	5	4	7
7	4	8	2	1	5	9	3	6
6	9	5	4	7	3	8	1	2

PUZZLE 13

7	2	4	6	3	5	8	9	1
3	8	1	7	2	9	5	4	6
6	5	9	4	8	1	3	2	7
8	4	7	1	9	6	2	5	3
5	6	3	8	4	2	1	7	9
9	1	2	5	7	3	6	8	4
1	7	8	2	6	4	9	3	5
2	9	6	3	5	7	4	1	8
4	3	5	9	1	8	7	6	2

PUZZLE 14

8	2	6	1	5	7	9	4	3
7	3	9	2	4	8	6	1	5
4	1	5	9	6	3	2	7	8
5	7	2	8	9	6	1	3	4
6	8	3	4	1	5	7	2	9
9	4	1	7	3	2	5	8	6
2	6	7	5	8	4	3	9	1
3	9	8	6	7	1	4	5	2
1	5	4	3	2	9	8	6	7

PUZZLE 15

4	6	5	7	1	3	9	8	2
1	8	3	2	9	4	5	7	6
7	9	2	8	6	5	1	3	4
2	4	1	6	7	8	3	9	5
5	7	9	4	3	1	6	2	8
8	3	6	9	5	2	7	4	1
6	1	4	3	8	7	2	5	9
9	2	7	5	4	6	8	1	3
3	5	8	1	2	9	4	6	7

PUZZLE 16

Z	I	N	M	B	E	H	O	R
M	O	B	H	N	R	I	E	Z
E	R	H	O	I	Z	M	B	N
H	M	O	E	R	N	B	Z	I
N	E	I	B	Z	O	R	M	H
B	Z	R	I	M	H	O	N	E
O	H	Z	R	E	M	N	I	B
R	B	E	N	O	I	Z	H	M
I	N	M	Z	H	B	E	R	O

ANSWERS

PUZZLE 17

O	L	K	I	G	N	S	H	D
I	H	G	D	O	S	K	L	N
N	D	S	H	L	K	G	O	I
L	S	I	O	N	G	D	K	H
H	N	O	K	D	L	I	S	G
G	K	D	S	I	H	O	N	L
D	O	L	N	S	I	H	G	K
K	I	N	G	H	O	L	D	S
S	G	H	L	K	D	N	I	O

PUZZLE 18

8	5	2	3	4	7	6	9	1
4	1	7	9	8	6	2	5	3
3	6	9	5	1	2	7	8	4
1	4	5	8	7	9	3	6	2
9	7	3	6	2	5	1	4	8
2	8	6	1	3	4	5	7	9
6	3	4	2	5	8	9	1	7
7	9	1	4	6	3	8	2	5
5	2	8	7	9	1	4	3	6

PUZZLE 19

4	5	3	9	8	7	6	1	2
6	7	2	1	4	3	9	5	8
1	9	8	6	2	5	4	7	3
2	1	7	4	3	6	5	8	9
3	8	9	5	7	1	2	4	6
5	4	6	2	9	8	1	3	7
7	6	4	3	5	9	8	2	1
8	2	1	7	6	4	3	9	5
9	3	5	8	1	2	7	6	4

PUZZLE 20

9	6	7	5	4	3	8	1	2
3	5	1	2	8	9	7	6	4
4	2	8	1	6	7	3	5	9
6	7	5	3	9	4	2	8	1
2	8	4	7	1	5	9	3	6
1	3	9	6	2	8	4	7	5
5	9	6	8	7	2	1	4	3
7	4	3	9	5	1	6	2	8
8	1	2	4	3	6	5	9	7

PUZZLE 21

3	6	5	9	1	7	2	4	8
8	7	4	5	2	6	3	1	9
9	2	1	8	3	4	5	7	6
6	1	8	2	7	5	9	3	4
7	3	2	4	6	9	8	5	1
4	5	9	1	8	3	6	2	7
5	4	7	3	9	8	1	6	2
1	8	6	7	5	2	4	9	3
2	9	3	6	4	1	7	8	5

PUZZLE 22

W	R	L	T	A	I	M	K	E
A	K	M	L	W	E	T	I	R
T	E	I	K	R	M	A	W	L
E	L	A	I	K	R	W	M	T
R	I	K	W	M	T	L	E	A
M	W	T	E	L	A	K	R	I
I	M	R	A	T	K	E	L	W
L	A	E	M	I	W	R	T	K
K	T	W	R	E	L	I	A	M

PUZZLE 23

Y	H	E	I	L	N	D	O	W
D	N	O	E	W	Y	L	H	I
W	I	L	D	H	O	N	E	Y
E	Y	W	N	D	H	O	I	L
L	D	N	O	I	W	E	Y	H
I	O	H	Y	E	L	W	D	N
H	E	I	L	N	D	Y	W	O
N	W	Y	H	O	E	I	L	D
O	L	D	W	Y	I	H	N	E

PUZZLE 24

4	5	1	2	9	8	6	7	3
8	6	3	4	5	7	9	2	1
9	7	2	1	6	3	8	5	4
1	4	9	6	2	5	7	3	8
6	8	5	7	3	9	1	4	2
2	3	7	8	4	1	5	9	6
7	1	4	9	8	2	3	6	5
3	9	6	5	1	4	2	8	7
5	2	8	3	7	6	4	1	9

3	9	4	2	7	6	1	5	8
1	5	2	4	3	8	9	6	7
7	6	8	9	1	5	4	3	2
9	8	5	3	6	4	2	7	1
4	1	3	8	2	7	6	9	5
6	2	7	1	5	9	3	8	4
2	7	9	6	8	1	5	4	3
8	3	6	5	4	2	7	1	9
5	4	1	7	9	3	8	2	6

PUZZLE 25

4	9	6	1	5	2	8	3	7
2	7	1	3	8	6	9	4	5
3	8	5	7	9	4	6	2	1
8	6	9	4	1	7	2	5	3
7	2	4	8	3	5	1	9	6
1	5	3	2	6	9	7	8	4
6	1	8	5	2	3	4	7	9
5	4	2	9	7	1	3	6	8
9	3	7	6	4	8	5	1	2

PUZZLE 26

6	5	7	4	9	8	1	2	3
8	2	4	3	7	1	5	9	6
1	9	3	5	2	6	4	8	7
2	3	6	9	1	7	8	4	5
7	4	5	8	3	2	6	1	9
9	8	1	6	4	5	7	3	2
4	7	8	2	5	9	3	6	1
5	6	2	1	8	3	9	7	4
3	1	9	7	6	4	2	5	8

PUZZLE 27

R	G	E	O	S	U	V	I	F
I	S	V	R	E	F	G	U	O
F	O	U	V	I	G	E	S	R
S	I	R	E	F	V	U	O	G
U	V	F	G	R	O	S	E	I
G	E	O	S	U	I	R	F	V
V	U	G	I	O	S	F	R	E
O	R	S	F	V	E	I	G	U
E	F	I	U	G	R	O	V	S

PUZZLE 28

H	A	O	P	M	F	I	R	E
P	I	F	H	R	E	O	M	A
E	R	M	O	I	A	F	H	P
M	P	A	I	F	R	E	O	H
O	F	R	E	P	H	A	I	M
I	H	E	M	A	O	P	F	R
R	E	H	A	O	I	M	P	F
F	M	I	R	E	P	H	A	O
A	O	P	F	H	M	R	E	I

PUZZLE 29

3	7	9	4	8	6	2	5	1
6	8	2	1	9	5	4	7	3
4	1	5	7	2	3	8	6	9
8	4	7	2	3	1	5	9	6
9	5	6	8	7	4	3	1	2
2	3	1	5	6	9	7	8	4
5	6	8	3	1	2	9	4	7
1	2	4	9	5	7	6	3	8
7	9	3	6	4	8	1	2	5

PUZZLE 30

3	5	8	7	2	4	9	1	6
7	2	1	9	6	3	8	5	4
9	6	4	1	8	5	2	3	7
6	3	2	4	5	9	7	8	1
1	4	5	3	7	8	6	2	9
8	7	9	6	1	2	5	4	3
5	1	7	8	3	6	4	9	2
4	8	6	2	9	1	3	7	5
2	9	3	5	4	7	1	6	8

PUZZLE 31

9	3	1	7	8	2	4	6	5
7	6	8	4	5	1	3	9	2
5	4	2	9	6	3	8	1	7
2	1	3	5	4	8	9	7	6
4	8	9	6	2	7	5	3	1
6	5	7	3	1	9	2	8	4
1	2	5	8	3	6	7	4	9
8	7	6	2	9	4	1	5	3
3	9	4	1	7	5	6	2	8

PUZZLE 32

ANSWERS

PUZZLE 33

S	C	I	D	O	U	M	N	E
U	D	N	M	C	E	S	I	O
O	M	E	I	N	S	D	C	U
D	E	M	S	I	C	U	O	N
N	S	C	U	E	O	I	D	M
I	U	O	N	D	M	C	E	S
E	I	S	C	U	N	O	M	D
M	O	D	E	S	I	N	U	C
C	N	U	O	M	D	E	S	I

PUZZLE 34

S	N	H	O	Y	D	R	A	U
Y	O	U	R	H	A	N	D	S
D	R	A	U	S	N	Y	H	O
R	A	O	Y	D	S	H	U	N
U	Y	N	H	A	O	D	S	R
H	S	D	N	R	U	A	O	Y
A	D	Y	S	O	R	U	N	H
N	H	S	A	U	Y	O	R	D
O	U	R	D	N	H	S	Y	A

PUZZLE 35

5	4	6	1	9	2	7	3	8
3	9	7	4	5	8	2	1	6
8	2	1	7	3	6	9	4	5
1	5	2	8	4	9	6	7	3
9	3	8	6	7	1	5	2	4
6	7	4	5	2	3	8	9	1
7	1	9	3	6	5	4	8	2
4	6	3	2	8	7	1	5	9
2	8	5	9	1	4	3	6	7

PUZZLE 36

4	7	1	3	5	2	9	6	8
3	5	2	8	6	9	4	1	7
9	6	8	1	7	4	3	5	2
7	9	5	4	2	1	8	3	6
6	2	3	9	8	5	7	4	1
8	1	4	6	3	7	2	9	5
1	4	7	2	9	6	5	8	3
2	8	6	5	4	3	1	7	9
5	3	9	7	1	8	6	2	4

PUZZLE 37

1	7	3	5	4	6	9	2	8
2	9	8	1	3	7	4	6	5
4	6	5	2	8	9	1	7	3
8	5	6	3	9	2	7	4	1
7	3	4	6	1	8	5	9	2
9	1	2	4	7	5	8	3	6
5	4	9	8	6	3	2	1	7
3	2	1	7	5	4	6	8	9
6	8	7	9	2	1	3	5	4

PUZZLE 38

L	T	Y	N	I	O	E	S	U
E	I	O	Y	U	S	T	L	N
S	N	U	L	E	T	O	I	Y
T	E	S	O	Y	N	I	U	L
O	Y	I	U	L	E	S	N	T
N	U	L	T	S	I	Y	E	O
U	L	E	I	O	Y	N	T	S
I	O	N	S	T	U	L	Y	E
Y	S	T	E	N	L	U	O	I

PUZZLE 39

J	D	U	I	A	O	H	N	L
O	A	N	J	L	H	I	D	U
H	L	I	U	N	D	J	O	A
U	H	A	O	I	N	L	J	D
N	O	D	L	U	J	A	H	I
I	J	L	H	D	A	O	U	N
L	I	O	N	J	U	D	A	H
A	U	J	D	H	L	N	I	O
D	N	H	A	O	I	U	L	J

PUZZLE 40

7	8	5	6	1	9	4	3	2
4	2	9	3	7	8	5	6	1
3	1	6	5	2	4	8	9	7
9	5	8	1	4	7	3	2	6
6	7	4	2	9	3	1	5	8
1	3	2	8	5	6	9	7	4
2	6	3	9	8	1	7	4	5
5	4	1	7	3	2	6	8	9
8	9	7	4	6	5	2	1	3

Fun BIBLE SUDOKU 2

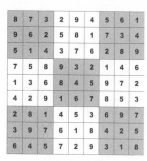

PUZZLE 41

6	3	8	9	2	5	1	7	4
4	2	1	3	7	6	5	8	9
5	9	7	1	8	4	6	2	3
3	4	9	6	5	2	8	1	7
1	8	6	4	9	7	2	3	5
7	5	2	8	3	1	9	4	6
2	6	5	7	4	8	3	9	1
8	7	3	5	1	9	4	6	2
9	1	4	2	6	3	7	5	8

PUZZLE 42

8	7	3	2	9	4	5	6	1
9	6	2	5	8	1	7	3	4
5	1	4	3	7	6	2	8	9
7	5	8	9	3	2	1	4	6
1	3	6	8	4	5	9	7	2
4	2	9	1	6	7	8	5	3
2	8	1	4	5	3	6	9	7
3	9	7	6	1	8	4	2	5
6	4	5	7	2	9	3	1	8

PUZZLE 43

4	1	9	8	7	6	2	5	3
8	2	6	5	9	3	7	4	1
7	5	3	2	4	1	8	9	6
5	7	2	9	6	4	3	1	8
6	4	8	3	1	2	9	7	5
9	3	1	7	5	8	4	6	2
3	9	5	1	2	7	6	8	4
1	8	4	6	3	9	5	2	7
2	6	7	4	8	5	1	3	9

PUZZLE 44

M	R	E	H	O	I	F	A	P
P	H	A	R	F	M	I	O	E
I	O	F	P	E	A	M	H	R
H	I	R	A	P	O	E	F	M
F	P	M	I	H	E	O	R	A
A	E	O	M	R	F	P	I	H
E	M	I	F	A	H	R	P	O
O	A	P	E	I	R	H	M	F
R	F	H	O	M	P	A	E	I

PUZZLE 45

O	I	R	W	U	N	Y	S	G
N	S	G	I	O	Y	U	W	R
U	Y	W	S	R	G	O	I	N
S	N	Y	U	G	W	I	R	O
R	U	I	O	N	S	G	Y	W
W	G	O	Y	I	R	S	N	U
I	W	N	G	S	U	R	O	Y
G	R	S	N	Y	O	W	U	I
Y	O	U	R	W	I	N	G	S

PUZZLE 46

3	2	5	8	4	1	6	9	7
4	7	1	6	5	9	3	2	8
6	9	8	2	7	3	1	5	4
2	3	4	7	9	5	8	6	1
5	8	9	3	1	6	4	7	2
7	1	6	4	8	2	9	3	5
9	4	2	5	3	8	7	1	6
1	6	7	9	2	4	5	8	3
8	5	3	1	6	7	2	4	9

PUZZLE 47

7	6	4	3	9	5	8	1	2
9	2	3	7	8	1	5	4	6
1	5	8	2	6	4	9	3	7
6	9	1	5	7	8	3	2	4
3	8	7	4	2	6	1	5	9
5	4	2	1	3	9	6	7	8
8	7	5	6	1	2	4	9	3
2	1	6	9	4	3	7	8	5
4	3	9	8	5	7	2	6	1

PUZZLE 48

9	2	4	1	8	5	6	7	3
3	5	6	9	7	2	1	8	4
1	8	7	4	3	6	9	5	2
6	4	5	2	1	3	8	9	7
7	9	8	6	5	4	2	3	1
2	1	3	7	9	8	4	6	5
4	7	9	3	6	1	5	2	8
5	3	1	8	2	9	7	4	6
8	6	2	5	4	7	3	1	9

ANSWERS

PUZZLE 49

6	8	2	9	5	3	7	4	1
4	9	7	8	2	1	5	3	6
5	1	3	4	7	6	8	9	2
2	5	8	1	4	7	3	6	9
9	6	1	2	3	5	4	8	7
3	7	4	6	9	8	1	2	5
1	2	5	3	6	4	9	7	8
8	4	6	7	1	9	2	5	3
7	3	9	5	8	2	6	1	4

PUZZLE 50

R	E	S	O	N	B	M	G	I
B	N	I	M	G	R	E	O	S
O	M	G	S	E	I	R	N	B
S	G	E	I	R	N	O	B	M
I	R	O	B	M	G	S	E	N
M	B	N	E	O	S	I	R	G
E	S	M	N	B	O	G	I	R
G	O	B	R	I	M	N	S	E
N	I	R	G	S	E	B	M	O

PUZZLE 51

A	T	P	N	G	S	E	I	Y
I	N	S	E	Y	A	G	P	T
E	G	Y	P	T	I	A	N	S
G	A	N	S	E	T	P	Y	I
Y	S	I	G	P	N	T	A	E
T	P	E	A	I	Y	N	S	G
N	E	T	Y	S	P	I	G	A
P	Y	G	I	A	E	S	T	N
S	I	A	T	N	G	Y	E	P

PUZZLE 52

2	7	3	8	1	5	4	6	9
5	1	4	2	9	6	3	7	8
6	9	8	3	4	7	5	2	1
4	6	1	5	3	9	2	8	7
7	3	2	6	8	1	9	5	4
9	8	5	7	2	4	6	1	3
8	4	6	1	5	3	7	9	2
3	2	7	9	6	8	1	4	5
1	5	9	4	7	2	8	3	6

PUZZLE 53

3	7	4	1	8	9	5	2	6
8	6	9	2	5	3	7	4	1
1	2	5	4	7	6	8	9	3
7	4	2	6	9	8	1	3	5
9	5	3	7	1	2	4	6	8
6	1	8	5	3	4	2	7	9
5	9	7	3	2	1	6	8	4
2	8	6	9	4	5	3	1	7
4	3	1	8	6	7	9	5	2

PUZZLE 54

5	6	8	9	7	3	2	1	4
4	3	7	2	1	5	6	9	8
9	1	2	6	4	8	5	3	7
1	4	6	7	9	2	8	5	3
7	5	9	3	8	4	1	6	2
2	8	3	1	5	6	7	4	9
6	2	1	8	3	9	4	7	5
8	9	4	5	6	7	3	2	1
3	7	5	4	2	1	9	8	6

PUZZLE 55

6	9	1	2	8	7	5	3	4
2	8	7	3	5	4	9	6	1
4	3	5	1	9	6	2	8	7
3	1	2	8	7	9	4	5	6
7	5	9	6	4	1	8	2	3
8	6	4	5	2	3	7	1	9
5	4	6	7	1	8	3	9	2
9	2	3	4	6	5	1	7	8
1	7	8	9	3	2	6	4	5

PUZZLE 56

W	I	S	M	O	R	H	E	P
O	E	P	I	H	S	R	M	W
R	H	M	P	E	W	S	I	O
S	O	R	E	I	M	P	W	H
H	M	E	W	R	P	I	O	S
I	P	W	H	S	O	E	R	M
P	S	O	R	W	E	M	H	I
M	R	I	O	P	H	W	S	E
E	W	H	S	M	I	O	P	R

Fᴜɴ BIBLE **SUDOKU 2**

PUZZLE 57

A	B	O	L	I	G	T	Y	H
T	L	I	Y	H	O	B	G	A
Y	H	G	T	B	A	L	I	O
L	A	H	O	G	I	Y	T	B
I	G	T	A	Y	B	O	H	L
O	Y	B	H	T	L	I	A	G
B	T	Y	G	L	H	A	O	I
H	I	A	B	O	Y	G	L	T
G	O	L	I	A	T	H	B	Y

PUZZLE 58

9	7	1	5	4	8	2	6	3
4	6	5	2	3	7	1	8	9
8	3	2	6	9	1	7	5	4
7	2	6	4	1	9	5	3	8
1	8	3	7	5	6	4	9	2
5	4	9	3	8	2	6	1	7
3	1	4	8	2	5	9	7	6
6	9	8	1	7	4	3	2	5
2	5	7	9	6	3	8	4	1

PUZZLE 59

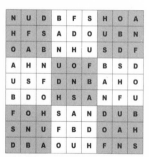

6	1	4	7	9	2	5	3	8
2	7	8	6	5	3	4	9	1
9	3	5	4	1	8	2	6	7
8	6	3	1	4	5	7	2	9
4	2	9	8	7	6	3	1	5
7	5	1	3	2	9	8	4	6
3	9	7	5	6	4	1	8	2
5	8	6	2	3	1	9	7	4
1	4	2	9	8	7	6	5	3

PUZZLE 60

2	1	4	9	6	3	5	7	8
5	8	3	1	7	2	6	9	4
9	6	7	5	4	8	3	1	2
4	3	6	8	5	1	7	2	9
8	2	9	7	3	4	1	5	6
7	5	1	6	2	9	8	4	3
6	9	8	2	1	7	4	3	5
1	4	5	3	9	6	2	8	7
3	7	2	4	8	5	9	6	1

PUZZLE 61

N	U	D	B	F	S	H	O	A
H	F	S	A	D	O	U	B	N
O	A	B	N	H	U	S	D	F
A	H	N	U	O	F	B	S	D
U	S	F	D	N	B	A	H	O
B	D	O	H	S	A	N	F	U
F	O	H	S	A	N	D	U	B
S	N	U	F	B	D	O	A	H
D	B	A	O	U	H	F	N	S

PUZZLE 62

E	S	F	A	O	P	N	I	R
R	N	A	S	I	F	P	O	E
P	O	I	R	E	N	A	F	S
I	R	E	O	N	A	F	S	P
O	F	P	E	R	S	I	A	N
N	A	S	F	P	I	E	R	O
A	E	R	N	F	O	S	P	I
F	I	N	P	S	R	O	E	A
S	P	O	I	A	E	R	N	F

PUZZLE 63

8	9	7	2	1	3	4	5	6
5	4	3	7	6	8	2	1	9
1	6	2	5	4	9	7	8	3
4	7	8	9	5	6	1	3	2
9	5	1	8	3	2	6	4	7
2	3	6	1	7	4	8	9	5
3	8	9	6	2	1	5	7	4
7	2	4	3	8	5	9	6	1
6	1	5	4	9	7	3	2	8

PUZZLE 64

6	2	8	5	9	1	3	7	4
3	4	1	6	8	7	9	5	2
5	9	7	3	4	2	8	6	1
2	3	4	9	6	5	7	1	8
8	7	5	1	2	3	4	9	6
9	1	6	4	7	8	5	2	3
1	8	9	2	5	4	6	3	7
7	6	2	8	3	9	1	4	5
4	5	3	7	1	6	2	8	9

ANSWERS

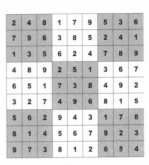

PUZZLE 65

3	9	4	1	2	6	5	7	8
7	8	2	5	4	9	6	1	3
6	1	5	8	3	7	9	4	2
5	4	3	7	1	2	8	6	9
8	6	1	3	9	5	7	2	4
2	7	9	6	8	4	3	5	1
1	5	8	2	6	3	4	9	7
9	2	6	4	7	8	1	3	5
4	3	7	9	5	1	2	8	6

PUZZLE 66

2	4	8	1	7	9	5	3	6
7	9	6	3	8	5	2	4	1
1	3	5	6	2	4	7	8	9
4	8	9	2	5	1	3	6	7
6	5	1	7	3	8	4	9	2
3	2	7	4	9	6	8	1	5
5	6	2	9	4	3	1	7	8
8	1	4	5	6	7	9	2	3
9	7	3	8	1	2	6	5	4

PUZZLE 67

L	E	M	A	O	T	H	W	R
H	A	O	R	E	W	L	T	M
R	W	T	H	L	M	E	A	O
A	L	H	E	M	R	T	O	W
W	O	E	T	A	H	R	M	L
M	T	R	O	W	L	A	H	E
O	R	L	W	H	A	M	E	T
E	M	A	L	T	O	W	R	H
T	H	W	M	R	E	O	L	A

PUZZLE 68

B	L	I	N	R	G	E	M	T
T	R	E	M	B	L	I	N	G
G	M	N	E	T	I	R	L	B
L	B	G	T	E	M	N	I	R
M	I	T	G	N	R	B	E	L
E	N	R	L	I	B	G	T	M
N	E	L	B	G	T	M	R	I
I	G	M	R	L	E	T	B	N
R	T	B	I	M	N	L	G	E

PUZZLE 69

9	5	3	8	1	6	2	4	7
6	1	2	3	7	4	9	8	5
4	8	7	2	9	5	1	6	3
1	3	6	4	8	9	5	7	2
2	7	9	6	5	3	4	1	8
5	4	8	7	2	1	6	3	9
8	9	4	1	3	2	7	5	6
3	2	1	5	6	7	8	9	4
7	6	5	9	4	8	3	2	1

PUZZLE 70

8	5	7	3	9	2	6	1	4
3	4	2	6	1	5	8	7	9
1	9	6	8	4	7	3	2	5
4	2	8	9	6	3	7	5	1
6	7	5	1	2	4	9	3	8
9	3	1	5	7	8	4	6	2
2	8	9	7	3	1	5	4	6
5	1	3	4	8	6	2	9	7
7	6	4	2	5	9	1	8	3

PUZZLE 71

1	8	7	4	3	9	2	6	5
6	9	4	2	5	7	8	1	3
5	3	2	8	6	1	4	9	7
4	2	1	3	7	8	9	5	6
3	6	9	5	1	2	7	8	4
8	7	5	9	4	6	3	2	1
9	4	6	7	2	5	1	3	8
2	5	3	1	8	4	6	7	9
7	1	8	6	9	3	5	4	2

PUZZLE 72

H	R	N	S	U	O	I	A	D
S	O	D	N	I	A	U	R	H
U	A	I	D	R	H	N	O	S
R	N	S	A	H	D	O	U	I
D	I	A	U	O	S	H	N	R
O	H	U	I	N	R	S	D	A
N	S	O	R	D	I	A	H	U
A	U	R	H	S	N	D	I	O
I	D	H	O	A	U	R	S	N

Fun BIBLE SUDOKU 2

PUZZLE 73

C	I	W	G	H	E	T	A	R
R	E	G	A	T	I	H	W	C
A	H	T	R	W	C	G	I	E
W	G	E	T	C	A	R	H	I
I	A	H	E	G	R	W	C	T
T	C	R	W	I	H	E	G	A
G	R	A	C	E	W	I	T	H
H	T	C	I	R	G	A	E	W
E	W	I	H	A	T	C	R	G

PUZZLE 74

6	3	2	1	8	7	5	9	4
8	7	9	2	5	4	1	6	3
1	4	5	6	3	9	8	7	2
7	1	8	9	4	5	2	3	6
2	9	6	3	7	1	4	8	5
4	5	3	8	6	2	9	1	7
3	2	7	5	9	8	6	4	1
5	8	4	7	1	6	3	2	9
9	6	1	4	2	3	7	5	8

PUZZLE 75

7	8	5	6	9	1	3	4	2
4	6	1	3	2	8	9	7	5
2	9	3	5	7	4	1	6	8
8	1	7	4	6	3	5	2	9
5	3	2	7	1	9	4	8	6
6	4	9	8	5	2	7	1	3
1	2	4	9	3	6	8	5	7
9	5	8	2	4	7	6	3	1
3	7	6	1	8	5	2	9	4

PUZZLE 76

1	8	3	2	5	6	7	9	4
9	2	7	8	4	1	6	3	5
4	5	6	9	7	3	1	2	8
7	4	2	1	9	5	3	8	6
5	3	8	6	2	7	4	1	9
6	1	9	3	8	4	2	5	7
8	7	1	5	6	2	9	4	3
3	9	4	7	1	8	5	6	2
2	6	5	4	3	9	8	7	1

PUZZLE 77

2	6	3	7	9	5	4	1	8
1	8	7	3	2	4	6	5	9
5	4	9	8	1	6	2	3	7
7	5	8	4	3	2	9	6	1
9	3	2	1	6	7	8	4	5
6	1	4	5	8	9	7	2	3
8	9	5	2	4	3	1	7	6
4	7	1	6	5	8	3	9	2
3	2	6	9	7	1	5	8	4

PUZZLE 78

A	U	D	W	T	R	E	N	S
T	S	N	A	E	D	U	R	W
E	R	W	S	N	U	T	A	D
R	A	U	T	D	N	S	W	E
W	T	S	U	A	E	R	D	N
N	D	E	R	W	S	A	U	T
D	E	T	N	R	A	W	S	U
S	N	A	E	U	W	D	T	R
U	W	R	D	S	T	N	E	A

PUZZLE 79

A	N	D	B	R	U	I	S	E
S	R	U	N	E	I	D	A	B
I	B	E	D	S	A	U	N	R
D	S	I	U	B	E	A	R	N
R	E	A	S	I	N	B	U	D
N	U	B	R	A	D	S	E	I
U	I	R	A	N	B	E	D	S
B	A	N	E	D	S	R	I	U
E	D	S	I	U	R	N	B	A

PUZZLE 80

8	7	5	3	6	4	1	2	9
1	6	2	7	5	9	3	4	8
4	3	9	1	2	8	6	5	7
5	9	8	2	7	6	4	1	3
7	2	3	5	4	1	8	9	6
6	4	1	9	8	3	2	7	5
2	1	7	6	3	5	9	8	4
9	8	6	4	1	7	5	3	2
3	5	4	8	9	2	7	6	1

ANSWERS

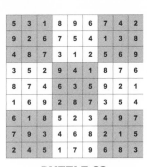

PUZZLE 81

5	9	1	4	8	6	2	3	7
2	3	8	7	1	5	6	4	9
4	7	6	9	2	3	5	1	8
7	6	5	1	3	8	4	9	2
3	8	4	2	5	9	1	7	6
9	1	2	6	7	4	8	5	3
8	5	9	3	4	2	7	6	1
1	4	3	8	6	7	9	2	5
6	2	7	5	9	1	3	8	4

PUZZLE 82

5	3	1	8	9	6	7	4	2
9	2	6	7	5	4	1	3	8
4	8	7	3	1	2	5	6	9
3	5	2	9	4	1	8	7	6
8	7	4	6	3	5	9	2	1
1	6	9	2	8	7	3	5	4
6	1	8	5	2	3	4	9	7
7	9	3	4	6	8	2	1	5
2	4	5	1	7	9	6	8	3

PUZZLE 83

6	5	8	3	1	7	2	4	9
1	9	7	2	5	4	3	6	8
3	4	2	9	8	6	5	1	7
9	6	4	5	2	8	1	7	3
8	7	3	4	6	1	9	2	5
2	1	5	7	3	9	4	8	6
5	3	6	8	4	2	7	9	1
4	8	9	1	7	5	6	3	2
7	2	1	6	9	3	8	5	4

PUZZLE 84

I	K	E	N	H	O	R	D	G
R	N	H	D	E	G	K	O	I
D	O	G	K	R	I	E	H	N
E	I	N	G	O	R	D	K	H
G	R	K	E	D	H	N	I	O
H	D	O	I	K	N	G	E	R
N	H	D	R	I	E	O	G	K
K	G	I	O	N	D	H	R	E
O	E	R	H	G	K	I	N	D

PUZZLE 85

R	H	O	M	U	E	F	I	T
I	U	T	R	O	F	M	H	E
M	F	E	I	H	T	O	U	R
F	I	R	E	M	O	U	T	H
T	O	M	H	I	U	R	E	F
H	E	U	F	T	R	I	M	O
E	R	H	U	F	M	T	O	I
O	M	I	T	R	H	E	F	U
U	T	F	O	E	I	H	R	M

PUZZLE 86

1	8	9	4	6	7	2	3	5
7	4	3	2	5	1	9	6	8
6	5	2	9	8	3	4	1	7
5	3	7	6	9	4	8	2	1
9	2	8	3	1	5	6	7	4
4	1	6	8	7	2	3	5	9
8	9	5	1	3	6	7	4	2
2	6	1	7	4	8	5	9	3
3	7	4	5	2	9	1	8	6

PUZZLE 87

1	6	5	9	8	4	7	2	3
2	4	3	6	7	5	9	1	8
9	8	7	1	3	2	5	4	6
3	7	4	8	9	1	6	5	2
8	5	1	7	2	6	3	9	4
6	9	2	5	4	3	1	8	7
7	1	9	2	6	8	4	3	5
4	2	6	3	5	9	8	7	1
5	3	8	4	1	7	2	6	9

PUZZLE 88

2	7	8	6	1	9	3	5	4
1	9	4	5	7	3	8	2	6
3	5	6	4	2	8	9	7	1
5	2	1	8	3	4	7	6	9
8	4	9	2	6	7	1	3	5
7	6	3	1	9	5	2	4	8
9	8	2	7	5	6	4	1	3
4	1	5	3	8	2	6	9	7
6	3	7	9	4	1	5	8	2

Fun BIBLE SUDOKU 2

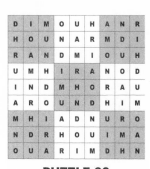

PUZZLE 89

D	S	N	T	R	A	O	E	V
O	T	R	V	D	E	A	N	S
E	A	V	O	N	S	T	R	D
S	N	E	D	T	V	R	O	A
R	D	T	E	A	O	S	V	N
V	O	A	N	S	R	D	T	E
N	V	S	A	O	T	E	D	R
A	E	O	R	V	D	N	S	T
T	R	D	S	E	N	V	A	O

PUZZLE 90

D	I	M	O	U	H	A	N	R
H	O	U	N	A	R	M	D	I
R	A	N	D	M	I	O	U	H
U	M	H	I	R	A	N	O	D
I	N	D	M	H	O	R	A	U
A	R	O	U	N	D	H	I	M
M	H	I	A	D	N	U	R	O
N	D	R	H	O	U	I	M	A
O	U	A	R	I	M	D	H	N

PUZZLE 91

3	4	5	7	6	9	8	2	1
7	1	6	8	5	2	4	3	9
8	2	9	3	1	4	7	5	6
6	3	7	1	9	8	5	4	2
2	8	1	5	4	3	9	6	7
9	5	4	2	7	6	1	8	3
1	9	3	6	8	5	2	7	4
4	6	8	9	2	7	3	1	5
5	7	2	4	3	1	6	9	8

PUZZLE 92

6	5	7	1	3	4	2	8	9
1	2	8	5	6	9	3	7	4
9	3	4	7	2	8	6	5	1
8	6	2	4	7	5	1	9	3
5	9	1	2	8	3	7	4	6
7	4	3	6	9	1	5	2	8
3	8	6	9	5	2	4	1	7
4	7	5	8	1	6	9	3	2
2	1	9	3	4	7	8	6	5

PUZZLE 93

7	4	3	9	8	2	1	5	6
5	6	2	4	1	3	9	7	8
9	1	8	7	6	5	4	2	3
1	9	6	8	5	7	2	3	4
2	8	4	1	3	6	5	9	7
3	5	7	2	4	9	6	8	1
6	7	9	3	2	1	8	4	5
8	2	1	5	7	4	3	6	9
4	3	5	6	9	8	7	1	2

PUZZLE 94

O	P	W	I	R	H	S	E	V
V	R	E	P	O	S	H	W	I
I	S	H	V	E	W	O	R	P
R	O	P	S	V	I	W	H	E
S	W	I	E	H	P	V	O	R
E	H	V	O	W	R	P	I	S
H	V	S	R	I	O	E	P	W
P	I	O	W	S	E	R	V	H
W	E	R	H	P	V	I	S	O

PUZZLE 95

H	T	D	R	N	A	M	E	O
O	E	A	H	M	D	R	T	N
M	N	R	T	E	O	H	D	A
N	O	H	M	D	R	E	A	T
D	R	E	O	A	T	N	M	H
A	M	T	N	H	E	O	R	D
T	D	O	E	R	H	A	N	M
R	A	N	D	O	M	T	H	E
E	H	M	A	T	N	D	O	R

PUZZLE 96

9	7	5	8	6	1	4	2	3
3	2	8	7	4	9	5	1	6
1	4	6	2	5	3	9	7	8
5	3	1	4	8	7	2	6	9
6	8	7	9	1	2	3	4	5
2	9	4	6	3	5	7	8	1
7	5	2	1	9	8	6	3	4
4	1	3	5	2	6	8	9	7
8	6	9	3	7	4	1	5	2

ANSWERS

PUZZLE 97

9	3	6	7	4	5	2	1	8
5	1	4	8	2	3	9	7	6
8	2	7	6	9	1	3	4	5
4	6	8	3	1	9	5	2	7
7	9	1	2	5	6	4	8	3
3	5	2	4	7	8	1	6	9
1	7	3	5	6	4	8	9	2
6	4	5	9	8	2	7	3	1
2	8	9	1	3	7	6	5	4

PUZZLE 98

7	6	3	5	1	8	9	2	4
8	2	5	3	9	4	1	6	7
1	4	9	7	2	6	3	5	8
3	9	8	1	6	2	4	7	5
5	7	2	4	8	3	6	9	1
4	1	6	9	7	5	2	8	3
2	3	4	8	5	9	7	1	6
9	5	7	6	3	1	8	4	2
6	8	1	2	4	7	5	3	9

PUZZLE 99

E	O	Y	R	B	T	M	L	A
A	M	B	L	Y	O	R	E	T
R	L	T	A	E	M	B	Y	O
O	R	L	Y	T	B	A	M	E
M	B	A	O	R	E	L	T	Y
Y	T	E	M	L	A	O	B	R
T	E	O	B	M	R	Y	A	L
B	Y	R	E	A	L	T	O	M
L	A	M	T	O	Y	E	R	B

PUZZLE 100

P	R	A	Y	T	H	O	S	E
O	Y	H	S	E	A	R	P	T
T	E	S	P	O	R	H	Y	A
S	P	E	O	H	T	Y	A	R
Y	A	O	R	P	S	T	E	H
H	T	R	A	Y	E	P	O	S
R	S	P	H	A	O	E	T	Y
A	O	T	E	R	Y	S	H	P
E	H	Y	T	S	P	A	R	O

PUZZLE 101

3	5	4	9	1	8	7	2	6
2	9	7	4	6	3	8	1	5
6	8	1	5	7	2	9	4	3
4	6	5	3	2	9	1	7	8
9	1	8	7	4	6	3	5	2
7	3	2	8	5	1	4	6	9
1	7	3	2	8	5	6	9	4
5	4	9	6	3	7	2	8	1
8	2	6	1	9	4	5	3	7

PUZZLE 102

5	2	4	8	1	6	3	9	7
9	3	8	5	7	2	6	1	4
6	1	7	9	3	4	8	5	2
2	9	1	6	5	8	4	7	3
7	6	3	4	9	1	2	8	5
4	8	5	3	2	7	9	6	1
3	7	6	2	8	5	1	4	9
8	5	9	1	4	3	7	2	6
1	4	2	7	6	9	5	3	8

PUZZLE 103

8	4	3	2	9	6	1	7	5
6	2	9	7	1	5	8	3	4
5	7	1	4	8	3	2	6	9
3	6	4	5	2	8	9	1	7
7	5	8	1	6	9	4	2	3
1	9	2	3	4	7	5	8	6
4	1	5	6	3	2	7	9	8
2	8	6	9	7	4	3	5	1
9	3	7	8	5	1	6	4	2

PUZZLE 104

T	I	R	O	A	H	W	F	V
O	V	H	F	T	W	I	R	A
W	F	A	I	R	V	T	H	O
R	W	I	A	V	F	H	O	T
A	H	V	R	O	T	F	I	W
F	T	O	H	W	I	A	V	R
I	O	W	T	F	R	V	A	H
H	R	T	V	I	A	O	W	F
V	A	F	W	H	O	R	T	I

Fᴜɴ BIBLE **SUDOKU 2**

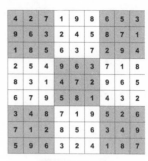

PUZZLE 105

T	V	O	S	H	E	A	F	R
F	S	E	O	A	R	T	V	H
A	H	R	F	V	T	S	E	O
V	E	T	H	S	O	R	A	F
O	F	H	A	R	V	E	S	T
R	A	S	T	E	F	O	H	V
E	T	A	V	O	H	F	R	S
H	R	F	E	T	S	V	O	A
S	O	V	R	F	A	H	T	E

PUZZLE 106

4	2	7	1	9	8	6	5	3
9	6	3	2	4	5	8	7	1
1	8	5	6	3	7	2	9	4
2	5	4	9	6	3	7	1	8
8	3	1	4	7	2	9	6	5
6	7	9	5	8	1	4	3	2
3	4	8	7	1	9	5	2	6
7	1	2	8	5	6	3	4	9
5	9	6	3	2	4	1	8	7

PUZZLE 107

3	4	6	1	7	5	2	8	9
8	7	5	3	9	2	4	1	6
1	2	9	6	8	4	5	3	7
5	3	2	9	6	7	8	4	1
9	6	4	8	2	1	3	7	5
7	1	8	4	5	3	9	6	2
4	9	3	5	1	6	7	2	8
6	8	7	2	4	9	1	5	3
2	5	1	7	3	8	6	9	4

PUZZLE 108

2	6	3	7	5	4	1	9	8
5	1	9	2	8	6	4	3	7
4	7	8	9	1	3	2	5	6
9	2	1	3	6	7	5	8	4
3	8	4	5	9	2	6	7	1
6	5	7	8	4	1	3	2	9
8	9	6	4	2	5	7	1	3
1	3	5	6	7	9	8	4	2
7	4	2	1	3	8	9	6	5

PUZZLE 109

A	O	U	S	T	L	E	H	D
S	L	E	H	U	D	A	T	O
D	H	T	O	A	E	L	S	U
L	T	S	U	E	H	O	D	A
E	D	H	L	O	A	T	U	S
U	A	O	D	S	T	H	L	E
T	U	D	E	L	O	S	A	H
O	S	L	A	H	U	D	E	T
H	E	A	T	D	S	U	O	L

PUZZLE 110

I	A	W	T	N	G	H	R	Y
T	G	H	Y	I	R	N	W	A
N	R	Y	H	W	A	T	G	I
Y	T	N	I	R	H	W	A	G
H	W	R	A	G	N	Y	I	T
G	I	A	W	T	Y	R	H	N
W	H	T	N	A	I	G	Y	R
R	Y	I	G	H	T	A	N	W
A	N	G	R	Y	W	I	T	H

PUZZLE 111

3	2	7	5	4	8	1	9	6
5	8	4	1	9	6	3	7	2
9	6	1	3	7	2	4	8	5
6	5	2	8	1	9	7	3	4
1	4	8	7	3	5	6	2	9
7	3	9	6	2	4	8	5	1
2	9	3	4	6	7	5	1	8
8	7	6	2	5	1	9	4	3
4	1	5	9	8	3	2	6	7

PUZZLE 112

9	4	8	7	1	2	6	3	5
1	3	6	5	4	9	7	2	8
5	7	2	3	6	8	9	4	1
3	9	7	4	2	5	1	8	6
2	6	5	8	7	1	3	9	4
8	1	4	6	9	3	2	5	7
4	2	9	1	8	6	5	7	3
6	8	3	9	5	7	4	1	2
7	5	1	2	3	4	8	6	9

ANSWERS

PUZZLE 113

9	6	8	1	7	2	5	4	3
4	5	3	8	9	6	2	7	1
2	7	1	5	3	4	9	6	8
8	3	4	9	6	5	1	2	7
7	1	5	2	4	8	3	9	6
6	2	9	7	1	3	4	8	5
5	8	6	4	2	1	7	3	9
3	9	2	6	5	7	8	1	4
1	4	7	3	8	9	6	5	2

PUZZLE 114

M	S	C	H	E	A	N	R	T
E	H	N	S	R	T	A	M	C
R	A	T	N	M	C	E	S	H
C	E	M	T	S	N	H	A	R
H	N	S	E	A	R	C	T	M
A	T	R	C	H	M	S	E	N
N	R	E	M	C	S	T	H	A
T	M	H	A	N	E	R	C	S
S	C	A	R	T	H	M	N	E

PUZZLE 115

S	N	R	E	T	A	O	M	H
O	A	M	H	N	S	T	R	E
T	H	E	R	O	M	A	N	S
M	R	A	O	H	E	N	S	T
H	T	O	N	S	R	M	E	A
N	E	S	A	M	T	H	O	R
A	O	N	S	E	H	R	T	M
R	S	T	M	A	N	E	H	O
E	M	H	T	R	O	S	A	N

PUZZLE 116

7	1	4	5	9	8	2	3	6
9	5	6	2	7	3	4	1	8
2	3	8	6	1	4	5	7	9
1	2	9	3	8	5	6	4	7
8	4	3	9	6	7	1	2	5
5	6	7	4	2	1	8	9	3
6	7	1	8	4	9	3	5	2
4	8	5	7	3	2	9	6	1
3	9	2	1	5	6	7	8	4

PUZZLE 117

7	8	2	6	9	1	4	3	5
5	4	6	3	7	2	1	8	9
1	9	3	4	8	5	6	7	2
4	1	5	8	2	7	9	6	3
9	2	7	1	3	6	5	4	8
3	6	8	5	4	9	7	2	1
2	7	4	9	1	8	3	5	6
8	5	9	7	6	3	2	1	4
6	3	1	2	5	4	8	9	7

PUZZLE 118

1	4	8	3	2	7	6	5	9
3	6	7	4	9	5	8	2	1
9	5	2	8	6	1	3	4	7
2	3	5	9	4	6	1	7	8
7	8	4	2	1	3	5	9	6
6	1	9	7	5	8	2	3	4
8	2	6	5	7	9	4	1	3
5	9	3	1	8	4	7	6	2
4	7	1	6	3	2	9	8	5

PUZZLE 119

S	O	U	R	D	I	N	F	W
N	F	R	S	U	W	I	O	D
I	W	D	N	O	F	S	U	R
D	I	W	O	F	N	U	R	S
R	U	N	I	S	D	O	W	F
O	S	F	U	W	R	D	I	N
W	D	S	F	I	U	R	N	O
U	R	O	W	N	S	F	D	I
F	N	I	D	R	O	W	S	U

PUZZLE 120

P	E	W	I	O	R	S	D	H
H	R	S	E	P	D	W	I	O
O	I	D	W	S	H	R	P	E
S	D	I	P	E	O	H	W	R
E	H	P	R	D	W	I	O	S
W	O	R	S	H	I	P	E	D
D	W	O	H	I	S	E	R	P
I	S	E	O	R	P	D	H	W
R	P	H	D	W	E	O	S	I

PUZZLE 121

6	4	8	9	5	1	3	7	2
5	9	2	3	7	4	8	6	1
3	1	7	2	8	6	4	5	9
4	3	9	6	2	8	5	1	7
8	2	1	7	9	5	6	4	3
7	5	6	4	1	3	9	2	8
1	7	4	5	3	9	2	8	6
9	8	5	1	6	2	7	3	4
2	6	3	8	4	7	1	9	5

PUZZLE 122

3	4	6	9	7	8	2	1	5
2	7	9	1	3	5	8	6	4
5	1	8	4	2	6	3	7	9
9	6	4	8	1	2	5	3	7
7	5	1	6	9	3	4	8	2
8	3	2	5	4	7	6	9	1
6	9	3	2	5	1	7	4	8
1	2	7	3	8	4	9	5	6
4	8	5	7	6	9	1	2	3

PUZZLE 123

1	5	8	4	2	9	7	6	3
6	7	9	1	8	3	4	5	2
3	2	4	5	6	7	8	9	1
5	6	3	9	4	2	1	7	8
7	8	2	3	1	6	9	4	5
9	4	1	8	7	5	2	3	6
2	3	5	7	9	1	6	8	4
4	1	7	6	3	8	5	2	9
8	9	6	2	5	4	3	1	7

PUZZLE 124

A	S	R	Y	I	O	E	D	P
P	O	E	S	R	D	I	Y	A
Y	I	D	E	A	P	S	R	O
E	P	I	O	S	R	Y	A	D
O	R	Y	I	D	A	P	E	S
D	A	S	P	E	Y	O	I	R
R	Y	P	A	O	I	D	S	E
I	E	A	D	P	S	R	O	Y
S	D	O	R	Y	E	A	P	I

PUZZLE 125

S	I	A	U	H	R	D	E	T
H	R	T	S	D	E	U	A	I
E	D	U	A	T	I	H	R	S
A	U	D	H	S	T	E	I	R
R	H	I	D	E	A	S	T	U
T	S	E	R	I	U	A	D	H
D	A	R	I	U	S	T	H	E
I	E	S	T	A	H	R	U	D
U	T	H	E	R	D	I	S	A

PUZZLE 126

6	3	1	7	2	5	9	4	8
8	4	7	9	3	6	5	2	1
9	5	2	8	4	1	7	6	3
3	1	6	2	7	9	4	8	5
7	2	4	5	1	8	6	3	9
5	8	9	4	6	3	2	1	7
1	9	3	6	5	4	8	7	2
2	6	8	3	9	7	1	5	4
4	7	5	1	8	2	3	9	6

PUZZLE 127

6	8	2	9	1	4	7	3	5
7	1	5	6	3	2	4	9	8
3	4	9	7	8	5	2	6	1
8	5	4	3	2	7	6	1	9
1	3	7	4	6	9	8	5	2
2	9	6	1	5	8	3	4	7
4	2	8	5	9	6	1	7	3
9	7	3	8	4	1	5	2	6
5	6	1	2	7	3	9	8	4

PUZZLE 128

E	L	I	P	D	S	A	O	C
P	C	A	O	E	L	D	I	S
O	D	S	A	C	I	E	P	L
D	O	E	I	A	C	L	S	P
S	I	C	L	P	E	O	A	D
A	P	L	S	O	D	C	E	I
I	E	P	D	L	O	S	C	A
C	S	D	E	I	A	P	L	O
L	A	O	C	S	P	I	D	E

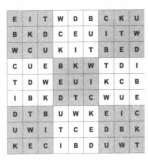

O	T	Y	E	U	R	B	H	A
B	R	E	A	T	H	Y	O	U
H	U	A	O	Y	B	E	R	T
U	E	O	Y	B	T	H	A	R
T	Y	R	H	A	E	U	B	O
A	H	B	R	O	U	T	E	Y
R	A	U	B	E	Y	O	T	H
Y	B	H	T	R	O	A	U	E
E	O	T	U	H	A	R	Y	B

PUZZLE 129

E	I	T	W	D	B	C	K	U
B	K	D	C	E	U	I	T	W
W	C	U	K	I	T	B	E	D
C	U	E	B	K	W	T	D	I
T	D	W	E	U	I	K	C	B
I	B	K	D	T	C	W	U	E
D	T	B	U	W	K	E	I	C
U	W	I	T	C	E	D	B	K
K	E	C	I	B	D	U	W	T

PUZZLE 130

A	R	U	I	F	D	L	E	G
F	G	E	L	A	R	D	I	U
D	I	L	U	E	G	R	A	F
R	A	F	G	L	I	E	U	D
U	E	G	D	R	F	A	L	I
L	D	I	A	U	E	F	G	R
I	F	D	E	G	A	U	R	L
G	U	A	R	D	L	I	F	E
E	L	R	F	I	U	G	D	A

PUZZLE 131

5	2	1	7	9	6	8	4	3
7	6	9	4	3	8	5	2	1
3	4	8	2	5	1	9	7	6
8	9	4	1	7	3	2	6	5
1	3	5	8	6	2	7	9	4
6	7	2	9	4	5	3	1	8
9	1	7	5	8	4	6	3	2
4	5	6	3	2	7	1	8	9
2	8	3	6	1	9	4	5	7

PUZZLE 132

5	9	6	7	4	2	3	8	1
4	7	8	1	9	3	6	2	5
2	3	1	5	8	6	7	4	9
1	5	4	2	7	8	9	3	6
7	6	9	4	3	1	2	5	8
8	2	3	9	6	5	1	7	4
9	1	7	3	5	4	8	6	2
3	8	5	6	2	9	4	1	7
6	4	2	8	1	7	5	9	3

PUZZLE 133

1	6	8	2	7	3	5	4	9
7	2	3	9	5	4	1	6	8
4	5	9	8	6	1	2	7	3
5	7	4	1	9	6	3	8	2
8	1	6	5	3	2	4	9	7
9	3	2	7	4	8	6	5	1
6	9	7	3	2	5	8	1	4
3	8	5	4	1	7	9	2	6
2	4	1	6	8	9	7	3	5

PUZZLE 134

C	O	S	E	R	A	U	T	H
T	H	E	C	U	S	A	O	R
U	R	A	T	H	O	C	S	E
A	S	R	O	C	H	E	U	T
O	T	C	U	E	R	H	A	S
E	U	H	S	A	T	O	R	C
S	C	O	A	T	E	R	H	U
H	A	U	R	S	C	T	E	O
R	E	T	H	O	U	S	C	A

PUZZLE 135

I	E	T	R	D	N	H	A	L
L	N	R	H	A	I	D	E	T
A	D	H	L	T	E	N	R	I
T	H	E	I	R	L	A	N	D
D	L	N	E	H	A	I	T	R
R	I	A	T	N	D	E	L	H
N	R	L	D	E	H	T	I	A
E	T	D	A	I	R	L	H	N
H	A	I	N	L	T	R	D	E

PUZZLE 136

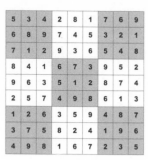

PUZZLE 137

1	6	9	5	2	4	7	3	8
7	5	3	8	1	9	2	4	6
4	8	2	7	6	3	1	9	5
3	7	6	9	8	5	4	1	2
2	4	5	1	7	6	3	8	9
8	9	1	4	3	2	6	5	7
9	3	4	6	5	7	8	2	1
5	1	7	2	4	8	9	6	3
6	2	8	3	9	1	5	7	4

PUZZLE 138

5	3	4	2	8	1	7	6	9
6	8	9	7	4	5	3	2	1
7	1	2	9	3	6	5	4	8
8	4	1	6	7	3	9	5	2
9	6	3	5	1	2	8	7	4
2	5	7	4	9	8	6	1	3
1	2	6	3	5	9	4	8	7
3	7	5	8	2	4	1	9	6
4	9	8	1	6	7	2	3	5

PUZZLE 139

2	6	5	7	1	4	9	3	8
8	7	1	6	9	3	4	5	2
9	3	4	8	5	2	7	6	1
3	2	8	9	4	1	5	7	6
1	4	7	5	2	6	8	9	3
5	9	6	3	8	7	2	1	4
6	8	2	1	7	5	3	4	9
7	1	9	4	3	8	6	2	5
4	5	3	2	6	9	1	8	7

PUZZLE 140

O	N	E	L	D	W	A	R	F
R	F	W	A	N	O	E	D	L
D	A	L	F	R	E	N	W	O
L	E	R	N	O	F	D	A	W
N	O	D	W	A	R	F	L	E
F	W	A	E	L	D	O	N	R
W	D	O	R	F	N	L	E	A
A	R	F	D	E	L	W	O	N
E	L	N	O	W	A	R	F	D

PUZZLE 141

W	A	S	H	U	N	G	R	Y
U	R	G	Y	S	W	A	H	N
H	Y	N	G	R	A	W	U	S
S	W	H	U	G	Y	R	N	A
A	G	R	S	N	H	Y	W	U
Y	N	U	W	A	R	S	G	H
N	H	W	R	Y	S	U	A	G
R	U	Y	A	H	G	N	S	W
G	S	A	N	W	U	H	Y	R

PUZZLE 142

9	5	1	4	2	7	6	3	8
6	7	3	1	8	5	4	2	9
2	4	8	9	3	6	1	5	7
4	1	7	2	9	8	5	6	3
5	3	9	6	7	4	8	1	2
8	6	2	3	5	1	7	9	4
1	9	6	7	4	2	3	8	5
7	2	5	8	6	3	9	4	1
3	8	4	5	1	9	2	7	6

PUZZLE 143

2	3	8	5	1	6	4	7	9
1	6	4	3	9	7	8	2	5
9	7	5	4	8	2	3	1	6
8	1	3	6	4	9	7	5	2
5	4	9	2	7	8	6	3	1
6	2	7	1	3	5	9	8	4
4	9	1	8	2	3	5	6	7
3	5	2	7	6	4	1	9	8
7	8	6	9	5	1	2	4	3

PUZZLE 144

7	2	1	8	9	6	5	4	3
3	9	4	1	2	5	8	7	6
5	8	6	4	7	3	2	1	9
4	6	2	5	1	9	7	3	8
9	3	5	7	8	4	6	2	1
1	7	8	6	3	2	9	5	4
8	1	3	9	5	7	4	6	2
6	5	9	2	4	1	3	8	7
2	4	7	3	6	8	1	9	5

ANSWERS

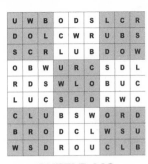

PUZZLE 145

C	F	H	M	E	A	T	O	U
A	U	E	O	H	T	M	F	C
O	T	M	U	C	F	H	A	E
H	O	F	T	M	C	U	E	A
E	A	T	H	O	U	C	M	F
M	C	U	F	A	E	O	T	H
T	E	O	A	U	H	F	C	M
U	M	A	C	F	O	E	H	T
F	H	C	E	T	M	A	U	O

PUZZLE 146

U	W	B	O	D	S	L	C	R
D	O	L	C	W	R	U	B	S
S	C	R	L	U	B	D	O	W
O	B	W	U	R	C	S	D	L
R	D	S	W	L	O	B	U	C
L	U	C	S	B	D	R	W	O
C	L	U	B	S	W	O	R	D
B	R	O	D	C	L	W	S	U
W	S	D	R	O	U	C	L	B

PUZZLE 147

9	8	1	2	7	6	5	3	4
2	6	3	5	1	4	8	9	7
5	7	4	8	3	9	1	2	6
7	2	5	9	6	3	4	8	1
1	3	6	4	8	2	7	5	9
4	9	8	1	5	7	3	6	2
3	4	7	6	9	5	2	1	8
8	5	9	7	2	1	6	4	3
6	1	2	3	4	8	9	7	5

PUZZLE 148

3	2	6	9	7	4	8	1	5
1	5	8	2	3	6	4	7	9
4	9	7	8	1	5	6	3	2
2	7	1	6	9	8	5	4	3
6	3	9	5	4	7	2	8	1
5	8	4	3	2	1	9	6	7
8	6	3	7	5	9	1	2	4
7	1	5	4	6	2	3	9	8
9	4	2	1	8	3	7	5	6

PUZZLE 149

5	4	8	3	7	1	9	2	6
2	1	7	6	5	9	3	4	8
9	6	3	4	2	8	7	1	5
3	2	5	1	6	4	8	9	7
1	9	6	7	8	5	4	3	2
8	7	4	2	9	3	5	6	1
6	3	2	5	4	7	1	8	9
4	5	9	8	1	6	2	7	3
7	8	1	9	3	2	6	5	4

PUZZLE 150

C	H	I	Y	T	P	E	R	O
T	Y	R	E	O	C	P	I	H
O	P	E	H	R	I	T	Y	C
E	O	T	P	I	H	R	C	Y
P	C	Y	R	E	O	I	H	T
I	R	H	C	Y	T	O	E	P
H	I	O	T	C	E	Y	P	R
R	T	C	I	P	Y	H	O	E
Y	E	P	O	H	R	C	T	I

PUZZLE 151

R	E	A	O	L	D	S	I	G
S	L	I	G	E	A	D	O	R
G	O	D	I	S	R	A	E	L
E	A	R	L	O	G	I	D	S
I	S	O	D	R	E	G	L	A
L	D	G	S	A	I	E	R	O
D	R	L	E	G	S	O	A	I
O	I	S	A	D	L	R	G	E
A	G	E	R	I	O	L	S	D

PUZZLE 152

5	2	9	8	1	4	7	6	3
7	8	6	3	2	5	4	9	1
3	1	4	9	7	6	5	8	2
6	9	3	7	4	2	8	1	5
4	7	8	1	5	3	6	2	9
1	5	2	6	8	9	3	7	4
9	6	5	2	3	7	1	4	8
8	3	7	4	9	1	2	5	6
2	4	1	5	6	8	9	3	7

PUZZLE 153

2	4	3	7	1	8	9	6	5
5	6	1	3	2	9	8	4	7
8	7	9	5	6	4	1	2	3
4	3	2	9	7	6	5	8	1
7	5	8	4	3	1	6	9	2
9	1	6	2	8	5	7	3	4
3	8	7	1	9	2	4	5	6
6	2	5	8	4	7	3	1	9
1	9	4	6	5	3	2	7	8

PUZZLE 153

PUZZLE 154

7	6	8	1	4	5	2	3	9
1	2	9	7	8	3	4	5	6
5	3	4	6	2	9	7	1	8
2	7	5	3	1	8	6	9	4
3	8	6	9	7	4	1	2	5
9	4	1	2	5	6	3	8	7
8	5	7	4	3	2	9	6	1
6	1	2	5	9	7	8	4	3
4	9	3	8	6	1	5	7	2

PUZZLE 154

PUZZLE 155

4	3	2	1	8	5	9	7	6
9	7	8	2	4	6	1	3	5
1	6	5	3	9	7	8	2	4
5	4	7	9	2	1	3	6	8
3	1	9	4	6	8	7	5	2
8	2	6	5	7	3	4	9	1
2	8	4	7	5	9	6	1	3
6	9	3	8	1	2	5	4	7
7	5	1	6	3	4	2	8	9

PUZZLE 155

PUZZLE 156

9	6	7	1	3	4	2	8	5
1	3	5	6	2	8	7	4	9
2	8	4	9	7	5	1	3	6
8	7	9	5	4	3	6	2	1
3	1	2	8	6	9	4	5	7
4	5	6	2	1	7	8	9	3
7	4	8	3	9	6	5	1	2
6	2	3	4	5	1	9	7	8
5	9	1	7	8	2	3	6	4

PUZZLE 156

PUZZLE 157

9	4	3	6	2	7	1	8	5
2	8	6	5	1	3	9	7	4
5	7	1	4	9	8	2	3	6
8	3	2	7	4	5	6	1	9
1	5	7	9	6	2	3	4	8
6	9	4	8	3	1	5	2	7
4	2	9	1	7	6	8	5	3
7	1	8	3	5	9	4	6	2
3	6	5	2	8	4	7	9	1

PUZZLE 157

PUZZLE 158

7	5	1	9	6	2	4	8	3
4	8	6	3	5	7	1	2	9
2	3	9	4	1	8	6	5	7
8	9	3	1	2	6	5	7	4
1	2	7	5	8	4	3	9	6
5	6	4	7	9	3	8	1	2
9	7	8	6	3	5	2	4	1
3	4	5	2	7	1	9	6	8
6	1	2	8	4	9	7	3	5

PUZZLE 158

PUZZLE 159

2	4	8	3	7	1	5	6	9
9	7	6	4	8	5	1	2	3
1	3	5	9	2	6	4	7	8
5	1	7	8	6	3	2	9	4
4	9	3	7	5	2	6	8	1
8	6	2	1	9	4	7	3	5
3	8	1	6	4	7	9	5	2
6	5	4	2	3	9	8	1	7
7	2	9	5	1	8	3	4	6

PUZZLE 159

PUZZLE 160

A	S	D	R	O	M	W	Y	N
W	N	O	Y	S	A	M	R	D
R	M	Y	D	W	N	S	A	O
N	O	M	A	R	Y	D	W	S
D	A	S	N	M	W	R	O	Y
Y	W	R	S	D	O	A	N	M
S	D	A	O	N	R	Y	M	W
M	Y	N	W	A	D	O	S	R
O	R	W	M	Y	S	N	D	A

PUZZLE 160